Dark Psychology Mastery

The Ultimate Collection To Master The Secrets Of Dark Psychology Using Covert Manipulation, Emotional Exploitation, Deception, Hypnotism, Brainwashing, Mind Games And Neurolinguistic Programming

–

Including Case Studies And DIY-Tests

By Patrick Lightman

Dark Psychology Mastery:

The Ultimate Collection To Master The Secrets Of Dark Psychology Using Covert Manipulation, Emotional Exploitation, Deception, Hypnotism, Brainwashing, Mind Games And Neurolinguistic Programming

Copyright © 2019 by Patrick Lightman

All rights reserved. No part of this book may be reproduced in any form including photocopy, scanning or otherwise without prior permission of the copyright holder.

Do you want to step up your People Analysis Skills and jumpstart your Decision-Making Game?

CLICK here to grab your Behavioral Science Cheat Sheet for FREE NOW.

Dark Psychology Secrets

Learn the trade's secret techniques of covert manipulation, emotional exploitation, deception, hypnotism, brainwashing, mind games and neurolinguistic programming

Introduction 7

Chapter 1: Welcome to the Dark Side 12

Chapter 2: Manipulation and Emotional Exploitation 27

Chapter 3: How to Sneakily Get What You Want 47

Chapter 4: Never Buy a Pig in a Poke 64

Chapter 5: Covert Take Overs 91

Chapter 6: Hostile Mind Takeover 124

Chapter 7: Playing Games 140

Conclusion 150

Dark Psychology Judo

How to spot red flags and defend against covert manipulation, emotional exploitation, deception, hypnosis, brainwashing and mind games from toxic people

Introduction 154

Chapter 1: Welcome to the Dojo 158

Chapter 2: Manipulation and Exploitation - Keep the Distance and Break Free 170

Chapter 3: Dark Persuasion – Keep Your Stance 190

Chapter 4: Deception – Spot the Attacks 210

Chapter 5: Covert Hypnosis - Keep Your Balance 233

Chapter 6: Brainwashing – Keep Your Stance .. 253

Chapter 7: Mind Games – Dominate the Battle Ground 272

Conclusion 292

Dark Psychology Secrets

Learn the trade's secret techniques of covert manipulation, emotional exploitation, deception, hypnotism, brainwashing, mind games and neurolinguistic programming

–

Including Case Studies And DIY-Tests

Patrick Lightman

Introduction

Welcome to the world of Dark Psychology. If you choose to stay, you will find out things you never knew existed. This is a journey not meant for the faint of heart. Secrets of darkness will be revealed, some of which you may find have been used against you.

The good news is that in this book, you will find ways to spot when dark psychology is being used on you or someone you care about. You won't be helpless against the darkness anymore. You will recognize it and know how to deal with it and the person attempting to dish it out.

I've become an expert on this subject due to all the research I've done to understand the powerplay and politics at top management level of Corporate America. One must delve into the sometimes wicked minds of executives in order to understand them after all. All the better for you that I've found out what lies behind the eyes of what seem to be innocent people.

With my newfound understanding, I found I had quite the different take on individuals I'd just met and even some that I already knew. And you will have this gift too *if* you decide to throw caution to the wind and go down this rabbit hole with me.

Whether you've always been one to see the best in this world or not, you will now find that every person may not be what they seem to be. Many people are out not only to take something from you but to try to keep you down if only to make them stand a little bit taller.

You know the type of person I'm talking about. The ones who seem to rise to the top, even though they've done nothing to deserve it. The people who tend to walk on others to get to the top. If you were aware of what they were trying to do, manipulate you into bowing down, letting them walk on your back, use you as a stepping stone, you would never allow it. These people mask their evil deeds. But soon you will know how to unmask these ruthless individuals. You will have the knowledge to deal with them on their own level.

Or maybe you will prefer not to deal with them at all. Learning how to harness your power and not allow anyone to take it is important too. You too can use dark psychology to help you get to the place you've always dreamt of getting to.

Why can't *you* have the top spot in the company? Why can't *you* have a beautiful home and a fancy car? Why can't *you* figure out how to rise above the crowd to stand out and get what you rightfully deserve?

The answer is simple.

People who know how to use dark psychology have already beaten you to the things you want and deserve. They know they haven't worked for it. They know they shouldn't have it or be in the position they're in. They do not care.

One can look at nearly every politician in office. Many know how to use dark psychology, and they keep using it to stay in positions of power. You see their faces on your television most days on the news. Maybe they're being discredited by others who follow the darkness. Perhaps others are attempting to – for lack of a better word – dethrone them. You won't see them fall, for they too know the secrets and understand how to bend the minds of people. All they have to do is make a select few believe in them, and then they will shake off the attack rather easily.

You, at home, are left wondering how they pulled it off. Soon, you will know how they did it. Soon, you will have the ability to move up if that's what you want to do. Soon, you will have the knowledge that will have you seeing the world in a different light - a light tinged with a darkness that you can learn to see and understand.

It's up to you how you will use this new power. Just remember that with power comes responsibility.

And karma is still a thing that one should watch out for, even if they are using the power of dark psychology.

So, are you ready to take a journey to the dark side?

Chapter 1
Welcome to the Dark Side

Handling Dangerous Knowledge

In this book, you will be given knowledge that is deemed dangerous. It would be remiss of me if I didn't caution you about the use of anything you find in these pages. Using negativity will only bring negativity upon you. You can understand darkness while not diving into it.

So let's understand what Dark Psychology truly is. It's not an exact science, more of an art form really. It is the study of mind control and manipulation of the mind. Manipulation in various forms is used. Coercion is when one uses threats to force a person into doing things they wouldn't normally do.

Manipulation is the art of making people think they actually want to do or say something that they really don't. Using insidious tactics to turn a person's mind around to benefit themselves is an unfair act that can leave the victim confused. They genuinely don't understand what made them say or do the thing they did. And all the while, the manipulator stands back, mouth closed, and eyes wide open, knowing what they did.

There is the power of persuasion that people using dark psychology can use. Somehow, they say all the right things to make the victim think in the terms they want them too. Gently, they lead the person to say things they wouldn't usually say and do things they never would've done.

And then we have motivation. The old, I'll scratch your back if you scratch mine scenario.

Dark Psychology is used in many ways in our society. I've pointed out how it's used in politics, but what about other places where large groups congregate?

Although it's not usually thought of as a thing that might use darkness to spread the word it's trying to spread; religions can use dark psychology to rein in its congregation. Some top religious authorities use the threat of hell to keep their followers in line.

One might wonder how terrorist groups get any followers at all. When the leaders use all sorts of dark psychology to brainwash people, it gets easier to understand.

Cults gain followers using the same techniques as everything else above does. So, when you get right down to it, wouldn't it be in your best interest to know and understand when someone is using these dark tactics on you or your loved ones?

I know I like the fact that I can easily see through the individuals who think they're so smart and can get anyone to do what they want, evil or not. And when they know that you can see right through them, they typically go away and leave you alone. There's no reason to even attempt to use their tactics on you if you're well aware of what they're doing.

This book is a powerful tool for those who read it. With knowledge, comes power. You will gain insight, you will be intrigued, and ultimately you will see things in black and white and know where you stand and where others do as well. Just make sure you use your new found knowledge for good, okay?

Beware of the Smiling Guy

Undoubtedly, you've met at least one of these smiling guys who just gives you the creeps right off the bat. Be thankful that you've got that innate sense – some people don't have it at all.

Criminologists and psychologists have something they use to pinpoint people who might have criminal or problematic tendencies. The Dark Triad is a list these professionals can use to gauge the magnitude or depth of the problems a person might have.

Here are the big three:

Narcissism is when a person has a rather massive ego. They boast about even the smallest achievement they've made – or claim to have made. They like to put on airs, also known as being grandiose. This gives them the appearance of being something they aren't. What the outside thinks matters to them a lot. They have no empathy. They don't care to understand where others are coming from or how things hurt them. And one of the craziest things they do is try to get others to empathize with them when they have no empathy for others. This is their world, and everyone in it are merely puppets to them.

Machiavellianism is the practice of deceptive manipulation. They want to use – exploit people to serve them and their missions. They have no moral character nor the morality most people are born with or, at the very least, are taught early on.

Psychopathy is a tricky one. These people can be the most charming people you've ever met. Politicians and religious figures, as well as cult leaders, fit this bill. But that charm isn't always there; it's used as a lure to get the victim into the lair where the person will impose their will on them once they're trapped.

Once they have control over their victims, they will begin to be impulsive. Said with the charm of being spontaneous, these people will impulsively do things without thinking about the outcome, or who might get hurt in the process. That's because they have a selfish streak a mile long. They too have no empathy for others, and what is worse, they don't have a remorseful bone in their bodies.

You have come across people with these three tendencies. There is no way you've lived even a small amount of time and haven't had to deal with one or more people who use darkness to bait you.

There are real-life cases of people who belong in the dark triad, and you meet them all the time. Take this case: I knew a man who hadn't worked but a short amount of time in his lifetime.

How is it that a man who had a wife and children and no disabilities managed to accomplish this feat, you ask? Using dark psychology is how.

He charmed and offered things he could never give, just to get others to put in what they could. Then he used what they'd provided, items intended to help the real unfortunate people he'd claimed he was gathering things for, for himself.

When he'd used up everyone around him, and they no longer would have anything to do with him, he played on the sympathy of his elderly mother. A woman on a fixed income whose husband had died years ago and left her in a home that was paid for, her husband, this man's father, knew he had to set his wife up, or their son would ruin her.

Guess what; he did anyway.

When the world he'd used turned on him, he went to his mother – told her that he was ready to end his life – he had nothing left to live for. His wife and children had turned on him, and now he was on his own.

Of course, no mother wants their child to end their life. So, she did what any parent would and asked what she could do to help. And boy was he ready with a list for her.

'A car, a place to live, three hot meals a day, Mom. That's all I'm asking for,' he pleaded. And she made sure he had those things, giving up her own car to him and giving him a room in her home, plus making meals for her poor, poor son.

One would think that would be enough, but oh no, not for the man who needed it all. Now he just needed to make money. And he couldn't go to work for anyone else because he was so much smarter than everyone else that it drove him crazy to work under people. He needed his own business -nothing big, nothing too expensive. All he needed was 10,000 dollars to make his lifelong dream – a dream his mother had never heard him talk about before – come true. That was all he needed. He could do the rest, and he'd pay her back with interest if that was what she wanted.

'Oh, no son,' she'd said. 'It's a gift to help you get back on your feet. I love you. I want to help you.'

So, he got the money, and for a very short time, he gave this business of his a shot. Not a real shot, a half-hearted shot. And he failed, and he came back to her home. He'd had to sell her car to have enough money to make it back to her home. He was back to square one and just needed a little more help. Maybe the church she used to go to before she got too weak to make it to services would be so kind as to help him.

And this went on and on, for a lifetime. People were used, abused, sucked dry and all for only one man to do nothing more with his life than be the guiltless, immoral, selfish vampire that he was.

At least you have this book. At least you have a way to spot people like this before they ruin your world or the world of someone you love. Because in this book, you will learn how to deal with people like this.

Wired for Deception

The reason the triad of dark personalities even exists in the first place is that we were born hardwired to listen to what people say and learn as well as develop from what's said. I don't care who you are; you weren't born knowing all you know or acting the way you do now. Your upbringing shaped you, and then you were shaped further by society after getting out into the world on your own.

Not every culture lies to their children, but some do. The myth of Santa and the Easter Bunny are characters that seem so real; children believe them to be true. When you add in that parents use these make-believe characters to get children to act right and be good, or they won't get presents or candy, you've got yourself an example of just how deceptive society is as a whole.

So, don't beat yourself up if you've ever fallen prey to many people out there who are trying to take something from you or have tried to make you see things the way they want you to. We've all fallen victim as well as have played the role of deceiver in our lifetimes.

Neuro-linguistic programming is a concept that some people came up with in the nineteen-seventies. You have an unconscious mind and a conscious mind. The two don't always seem to be speaking the same language at times.

As the name states, this deals with a person's neurology, linguistics – which is speech, and how to program these things to work for us. If you don't know how to communicate well with yourself, how can you do it with others?

Using NLP – a short term for that long word up there – one can talk to themselves and make themselves understand why we think some of the things we do and how to stop thinking about some of those things.

Here's a little example of how to go about this: I want to stop eating a whole pint of ice cream at a time. I've grown up watching my mother do this, and in my head, I think there has to be nothing wrong with it since she did it. But my weight and blood sugar levels tell me that there is something wrong with what I'm doing. I need to stop. I need to make myself believe that what I've seen from my mother wasn't the truth or right.

I have to have a heart to heart with myself about what is happening and what has happened in the past. I saw something, but that doesn't mean it was right. And this thing I saw may have hurt my mother's health too. She didn't communicate that to me. If she had, I might not have thought of eating all that ice cream at one time was a thing that was okay.

By talking back and forth with myself, I've concluded that my mother didn't think she needed to tell me that eating all that was unhealthy. She had her reasons. Possibly no one had told her about the harmful aspects of what she was doing. Who knows?

The thing is that I had a discussion with myself and taught myself that eating all that ice cream is unhealthy. Now that information is buried in my unconscious mind. And it's in my conscious mind too. So, if things worked right, the next time I go to grab the whole pint out of the fridge, I'll stop, get a bowl and a spoon and serve myself a reasonable amount of the cold, sugary treat.

DIY-awareness tests

Here are a few questions to help you think about what you've just read and learned.

1. If you were told by your parents that there is an Easter Bunny, does this mean you were raised by people with characteristics of the Dark Triad?

2. Can a used car salesperson exhibit characteristics of any of the big three neuroses that make up the Dark Triad? And what are they?

3. Have you been guilty of behaving in any of the ways that were mentioned in this chapter? And if so, then why do you think you acted that way?

Chapter 2

Manipulation and Emotional Exploitation

Why me?

Why do some people get taken advantage of and others don't? It seems like a crap-shoot, I know. But it's really not.

Everything happens for a reason. If you're gullible, then chances are there is something in your upbringing that made you that way. If you seek approval at all costs, chances are you couldn't find that in your childhood. As sad as it is, what happens to us in our younger years does more to shape us than anything else.

Some children are nurtured. They had stable families with no traumatic upheavals. And they seem to have it all together. Here's the deal; no one has it all together. But some have it more together than others.

If you're frequently the victim of manipulation, then you really need this book. You've got to learn to watch for signs of that whenever you're dealing with authority figures.

You may not fall for it from everyone, but you may have a harder time seeing it in people you're supposed to trust: your boss, your kids, and even your spouse. If people are often trying to sway you to their way of thinking or doing things for them that they should be doing for themselves, then you might have something you should be watching out for.

Here's an example of a person who is being manipulated or emotionally exploited:

Jane goes to work each day. She wants to do a great job and please her boss at all costs. One day, Jane is feeling ill. She's got a terrible headache and calls in to ask her boss for the day off. He tells her he can't spare her today, just come in and do your best.

Sounds reasonable, doesn't it?

Only when Jane gets into work, she finds there are two extra people who've been scheduled to work too. They're actually overstaffed. So, she goes in to tell her boss she really is feeling terrible and since the place is overstaffed, can she please have the day off? She understands she's giving up the pay for that day.

Still, he says he really needs her. She's a great worker. Sorry, she can't leave. And as a matter of fact, she needs to go scrape all the gum off the salesroom floor, and after that, the toilets really need a good scrubbing. And then he needs her to drive downtown to pick up his lunch. He's a diabetic, and this is the only place that has those sugarless twinkies he loves so much. It's his one treat for the entire day; he *so* needs it.

Jane doesn't say what someone who refuses to be emotionally exploited does. She bows her head, tells him she'll do it all and even thanks him before leaving his office.

She could've handled things very differently. She could've done things in a way that would've made her boss see that she wasn't a person who could be taken advantage of nor manipulated. With just a few words said differently, she could've stayed home and taken care of herself.

These words are simple and unfortunately people with the affinity to be emotionally exploited use them far too sparingly.

Here they are – *the magic words*: I'm sick, I won't be coming in today. (There is absolutely no reason to ask a question here. You are sick, and you won't be in – end of subject)

When asked to do something you feel uncomfortable doing, unsafe doing, or that it's not your responsibility to do, here is what you say: No. I will not do that.

When asked why you won't be doing it, here's the magic answer: Because I do not want to.

Now, if you've been giving in to this person for some time, then you can expect some negative feedback. They do think they can manipulate you after all. Don't let them say too much. Cut them off with some quick words of your own. Such as, you have my answer. Goodbye.

It takes practice but staying true to yourself over being true to anyone else is important, and you can do it. The way I think about it is like this. If I'm sick and someone wants to keep pushing me to work anyway, I ask myself, would you die for this SOB? Usually, my answer is no. Now, when it's a helpless little kid or a helpless elderly person, I suck it up and do what needs to be done. Other than that, it can wait, or someone else who isn't feeling sick can do it.

Here are some ways people can manipulate you or emotionally exploit you and how to handle each situation:

Love Flooding

This is when someone is buttering you up to get you to do something that they know you won't want to do. They may come and lather you with affection. Sweet kisses, hugs, nuzzles. "Baby, I love you. Can you get up and do my laundry really quick so I can stay in bed and sleep?"

Normally, you might be nice and do it. But last night you were up with the baby six times. And you've got an appointment with the dentist that you're not looking forward too after lunch. You don't want to get up and even start your day, much less someone else's – even if you truly love that other person.

Here is how you handle this sweet talk but still know that it's a manipulation:

"I love you, but our child kept me up, and I'm not looking forward to my day as it is, so no. You're on your own with your laundry, and as much as I love your affection, I'm not looking for any at this moment. I need my sleep. Night-night."

Lying

Most people can't abide liars – I'm one of those people. I will bend over backward for you, but if I catch you lying to me, then that's over and quick.

Lying happens a lot when someone wants you to give them some money. Here's an example and how you handle it without getting duped.

"I hate to ask, but I don't have a dime to my name, and little Susie has a terrible cold. The medicine is only ten bucks, but I don't have it. If I don't get some money, she'll suffer all night. And I don't get paid until Friday – that's three days away. I'm just worried about Susie is all, or I wouldn't even ask to borrow twenty bucks."

"I thought the medicine was ten dollars?"

"Yeah, it is. But while I'm out, I thought I'd pick up something to eat. You know, hamburgers, fries, a soda or two. Poor Susie is dying for her favorite junk food too. Poor baby."

All of a sudden, you see little Susie running around behind her momma's back, jumping off the furniture, laughing her head off.

Now is your chance to do what's right. So, you say, "She looks fine to me. I would've bought that child's medicine had she been sick. Don't ask me for money anymore." Then walk away without looking back.

Withdrawal

This is a hard one. When someone gives you the cold-shoulder or shuts themselves off to you just because you won't do what they want, then it hurts. I don't care who you are or how tough you might be. When someone turns away from you only because you won't do what they want, it's a terrible manipulation and the epitome of emotional exploitation.

It's easy to say, just don't let them get to you, but man, that's right at impossible. That is until you realize why they're doing it.

They want you to feel terrible for not giving in to them. They want to make you hurt. And for what?

Most of the time, what they wanted doesn't amount to a hill of beans.

Here's an example and how you should handle it:

You come into the living room, your arms full of groceries you need to unpack and put away. Your mother is sitting in the living room, doing her nails. 'Can you run out and feed my dogs, real quick?'

'I can't, Momma. I've got to put these groceries away, and I've got another armload in the car, then I've got to get to the school to pick up Ariel and get her to the doctor to get those warts of hers frozen off. Sorry.'

'My nails are wet. I wouldn't ask you if it wasn't important.'

'I'm sure your dogs won't die before your nails dry, and you can get out there to feed them, Momma. I really am in a huge rush right now.'

'It's just a small favor. You're being selfish. The dogfood is right there by the backdoor. You're right there by it. Now, put one scoop in pen for Fancy and then get a scoop out of the other bag for Bossy, he can't eat what Fancy does.'

'Mom, I know what they eat and how they eat it. I just don't have time right now. If you don't want to go outside, I'll feed them as soon as I get back home."

The bottle of nail polish goes flying. Nothing but the sound of stomping is heard as the room is vacated. The sound of a door slamming is the last thing you hear.

It's not the first time this has happened, and you know it won't be the last. What do you do? The last time she got mad like this, it was three days before she said one word to you?

I've lived this. I've dealt with this over and over on my life. My mother was one person who did this to me and my husband the other. I never learned how to deal with my mother, but you can bet I wasn't going to deal with this from my husband. So, I learned how to handle people who try to manipulate me by using this tactic.

Calmly, you go to where they've shut themselves off from you. You don't have to open the door, just speak calmly through it. "You're upset, that's plain to see. I am busy, that is also plain to see. You can pout, you can keep your distance from me, and you can keep your words to yourself too. You aren't hurting me if that's what you were going for. You're hurting yourself. You deny yourself human interaction." And then you walk away. You don't go do what she wanted you to do, you go on about your business, and if she's still not talking when you get back, you reiterate to yourself that she is only hurting herself, you can't be hurt by that.

Love Denial

Much like Withdrawal, love denial is when a person who loves you holds back that attention because you won't do something, they want you to. You can use the same type of scene from above to deal with that person. You will still talk calmly to them and let them know that what they are doing is only hurting them and not you. They are the ones who are missing out on love and attention by acting the way they are. You have to stay strong here and remain calm. They learned this. It was done to them. Have empathy for that, but don't tolerate it. Don't give in to it. They will learn that at least you won't be manipulated by this action.

Choice Restriction

Many of us have done this with our children. We offer only the choices that we want them to take while ignoring the one we know they really want.

For instance, little Sally is looking at the candy bars in the grocery store. We hold up grapes and apples. "Sally, you get to pick the treat today. Is it going to be apples or grapes?"

With only the two things to pick from, she's stuck.

But that's a child, and you're doing it for good purposes, not evil ones.

Now you're a grown person and you want to eat Chinese for lunch. You and your sister are in the food court at the mall and there are tons of choices. So, it stuns you when your sister says, "Oh, I don't want Chinese today. I'll let you pick though – Pizza or burgers? Go ahead. You get to pick."

I'm pretty sure there aren't lots of you who even need to know what to say here, but I'll put it out there, just in case.

You say, "Get a grip, sis. I'm getting Chinese. You get whatever the heck you want."

Reverse Psychology

Again, many of us have used this method of manipulation on our own children and even grown individuals to get them to see things our way.

You want your kid to put on their protective shoe coverings to go out into the rain. You know that your son hates to be told what to do. So, you say, "It's pouring out, but I don't see any reason for you to put your galoshes on over your new shoes. They should be fine."

"I don't want my shoes to get ruined, Mom. Gee whiz! I'm wearing them today."

You smile, mission accomplished.

But what if it's happening to you?

Your hubby would like his favorite shirt washed but doesn't want to do it himself. He says, "Aw, man. My favorite red shirt is dirty." He grabs up the red shirt and a handful of other clothes out of the hamper. Your white shorts and blouse are in the mix. "I'll just do a load. Don't worry, babe. I've got this."

You might be overlooking the obvious. He's hoping you will see the whites and stop him, take over, do the load yourself.

But you see what he's doing and stop him. "Oh, here let me take those whites. No reason for you to wash these with that red shirt, it'll turn them pink. There you go. You're good to go now, babe."

He's left frowning as his ploy did not work and you walk away with a smile on your face.

Semantic Manipulation

This one is pure torture. I am positive that you've said or been told, "I'm not going to argue semantics with you."

This is when someone wants to use your words, turn them into pretzels, and do their level best to drive you insane.

Think about any argument you've ever had with a child over doing their homework. "But I thought the teacher meant next Tuesday, not today. Why would they expect me to be able to turn it in with only one night to finish it?"

"Um, because it's only three lousy questions that would've only taken you ten minutes to finish."

You're out of your mind, and they're still trying to tell you what they thought.

Although it's nearly impossible to shut this type of thing down quickly, you must try. A calm voice never fails to get someone's attention. "Well, you were wrong about that. So, here it is in nice simple language for you. Do the questions now." Then walk away without saying another word. Don't listen to the rubbish that will surely pour from their lips, just keep on walking.

My best advice to you when you are faced with any type of manipulation at all is to walk away. Sometimes there are no words that will get through to a person. Sometimes you must just remove yourself from the equation.

If words are a thing you find necessary, say them with a calm tone, make it short and concise, and do not expect an answer. Walk away. Leave them on their own to think about what you said or did not say.

Most of all, remember that this is *their* problem, not *yours*. Don't let it become your problem.

DIY Exercises

1. You're busy at work, doing end of the month reports only you can do, when your boss comes in, tells you to put that to side, for now, he needs you to run an errand for him.

You can take the reports home to finish them on your own time. What do you tell him?

2. After you tell your husband that you can't stop what you're doing to cut his toenails right that minute, he storms out. What do you do?

3. Your son lies to you about where he was and when you try to get onto him, he yells at you that you lie too. What about the Easter bunny? What do you say?

Chapter 3

How to Sneakily Get What You Want

The power of persuasion is one way to get what you want. And it's not that evil to persuade people to do things, is it?

Advertisements are powerful persuasions. Everyone uses ads to get what they want. Politicians use them, and companies use them. we've even used persuasion to get you to buy this book. So how bad can it be, really?

When used for positive purposes, this power isn't anything bad. But when used for bad things, persuasion can get people into real trouble.

The Power of Positive Persuasion

When a friend has found something new, they really like and want you to join them.

"We went on a trip to the river last summer, Gail. I think you'd love it. You should come with us this year."

"I don't care for water."

"What do you mean, you don't care for water? Everyone loves water. And then there're these gorgeous sunrises and sunsets. You love those."

"I do love those. But the cost is probably much too high for me."

"Is free too high, Gail? I said you could come with us. And there's lots of fun to be had while floating down the river."

"Floating? Oh, no. It sounds dangerous."

"Donny is only five and can't even swim, and he floated down it with us. I think you'll find it safe, fun, and relaxing. Plus, we barbeque each night. You love Allen's ribs, don't you remember?"

"I do love his ribs. How long are we talking about?"

"A week."

"Oh, no. I can't be gone that long. What about my dog, Pookie? What would I do with her while we're gone?"

"She can come too. It's pet-friendly."

"Well, it seems you've persuaded me to go. Thanks, it sounds like it'll be lots of fun."

The Power of Manipulative Persuasion

"Folks, we've got some great deals for you. Step right up and let me tell you all about these steak knives we've got on sale now."

"I have a set already, thanks though."

"No, wait. You don't have *these* knives. These knives are a must for every household. You don't want to be the only guy on your block with cruddy steak knives, now do you?"

"Well, no. But mine are just fine."

"As fine as these. Just look at how they shine. And boy can they cut too. Just look at them slice through this thick steak."

"Well, that's pretty good. They are shiny. But I've got some. See ya."

"Wait. What if I told you that these are the same type of knives they use in the White House? They're good enough for our president and his family and the visitors that go eat with them. So, why aren't they good enough for you?"

"They are good enough for me. I just have some already."

"Why pass up this special offer? You don't know if you'll ever get this chance again. I'm only here for one day. I can't promise you that you'll ever get this chance again. It's the same knives as the White House uses. Don't you want to be a proud American?"

"Oh, heck. Give me a set."

The Power of Helpful Persuasion

"You should totally try this blush, Peggy. It'll look so good on you."

"Um, I haven't ever worn any makeup. I'm not sure how to put it on. I'll just make myself look like a clown if I try to wear any. Thanks though."

"Nonsense, you'd look great with makeup on as long as you don't use too much. I can help you if you want."

"I don't know. I've got this red hair, and my skin is so pale. I've never been able to find anything to match my skin tone."

"You have alabaster skin. It's like God's gift, Peggy. Come on, we can go to the store and I can help you pick out all the right things. For about a hundred bucks, I can get you all set up. And I promise to help you put it on and teach you how to do it so you can do it yourself. What do you say? You wanna let me help you be a better you?"

"Well, when you put it that way, how can I refuse? Thanks."

The Power of Gentle Persuasion

"Good afternoon, Jimmy. How was school today?"

"It was school." He tosses his school books onto the coffee table.

Mom looks at them. "So, do you have homework today?"

"Always," he huffs as he tries to leave the room.

But Mom has something to entice him into doing his homework now, instead of leaving it to the last minute, like he's always done. "I've got some cookies I've just baked. How about I get a plate of them and some nice cold milk and you and I can tackle your homework together? You know, get it out of your way?"

"Not now."

"You don't want any cookies?"

"What? Cookies? You said something about cookies?"

She gets up to go to the kitchen. "Yes, I'm going to get a plate of my freshly baked chocolate chip cookies and a couple of glasses of ice-cold milk. Why don't you take a moment to freshen up, splash some water on your face? I'll take the cookies and milk to the living room while you do that."

"That sounds nice, Mom."

Moments later they meet in the living room. Mom puts the things on the coffee table and picks up one of the books as Jimmy digs into the cookies and milk. "Oh, you have an assignment in biology today?"

"Yeah. It sucks."

"I used to love that class. Care if I take a look at the assignment?"

"Go ahead. Why should I care?"

Flipping to the marked page, she sees the assignment. "Whales, huh. Would you look at this? They live to be over a hundred years old. Can you imagine that?"

"Really?" He sits next to her, looking at the book with her. "How do they know how old a whale can get? Not many people live to be that old."

"Well, let's see." She reads the chapter out loud to Jimmy, who listens intently. And then she asks him the questions at the end of the chapter. "Maybe you should just jot the answers down to save you some time, Jimmy."

"Great idea."

With Mom's gentle persuasion, Jimmy got his homework done.

The Power of Sexual Persuasion

"I really should be going now."

"Why right now? We've got plenty of time."

"My laundry needs doing."

He gently caresses her cheek. "Laundry? I think you'll have time for that tomorrow, won't you? I thought we could open a bottle of wine and sit on the sofa and watch a movie together, just the two of us."

"Well, that does sound nice. But I really should be going. It's getting late."

"My bed has plenty of room if you'd like to stay over." He trails a line of kisses up one side of her neck. "I won't kick you in my sleep, I promise."

"Fluffy probably needs to be let out."

"Don't you have a litter box for your cat?" He snuggles closer to her. "I'm sure she'll be fine until the morning. And it's snowing outside. You really should stay. It wouldn't be hospitable of me at all if I sent you out in this kind of weather."

"I think I'll be fine."

"I can light the fireplace." Another trail of kisses flows over her face. "You'll be nice and warm here, in my arms, in my bed."

"Oh, boy, do you know how to persuade a woman!"

The Power of Bad Persuasion

"I started my diet last night."

"Good for you. Marsha. I wish I could find the self-discipline to start a diet too." Tatum picks up a donut from the box near the coffee pot at work.

Marsha stares at the gooey treat as her friend takes a large bite. "Yeah, I barely have had any cravings at all. So far."

"Wow, how great is that?" The donut drips some red jelly down Tatum's chin. "Oops."

Marsha hands her a napkin. "Here ya go, Tatum."

"Thanks." Tatum wipes her chin. "For lunch, me and some of the other girls from the office are all going to pitch in for pizza. Want to join in on the pizza party?" She puts her hand to her mouth as she raises her brows. "Oh, sorry. I forgot."

"Yeah, my diet doesn't allow pizza." Marsha holds up a brown paper bag. "I brought a salad and some celery sticks from home. Thanks for inviting me though."

Walking to her desk, she pulls a soda out of the drawer as Marsha makes herself a small cup of straight black coffee. "I can't stand that tasteless coffee. I've got to have my soda. I've got an extra can of it in here if you'd like it."

Looking forlornly at the can of soda Tatum shows her, Marsha slowly shakes her head. "It's not on my diet."

"What is on that diet anyway, Marsha? Twigs and berries?"

"Berries? I wish." Marsha sighs heavily. "I should get to work."

A few hours later, Tatum shows up in Marsha's office with one piece of pizza. "I saved you a slice. Come on, one slice of pizza won't hurt you, girl."

"I am starving." Marsha holds out her hand and takes the slice of pizza. "Thanks, Tatum."

Tatum looks at the bottle of water on Marsha's desk. "Here, girl. Have a soda too." She pops it open. "You only live once, right?"

And now Marsha's diet is a thing of the past, just that easily, thanks to Tatum's help and power of persuasion.

The Power of Evil Persuasion

"Look, Joe, everyone is doing it."

"Yeah, but I still don't think I should. My wife and I have a lot of trust in each other."

"She's out of town, Joe. What she doesn't know won't hurt her. You know what I'm saying? And that girl hasn't stopped looking at you since we came into this bar."

"Yeah, I shouldn't even still be here. I told my wife I'd get one drink with you guys from work then I'd get home and feed the dog. Butch is probably starving by now. I really should go."

"I ain't trying to be a buttinsky, Joe, but I've seen your wife. She's nice and all, but a little on the plump side and not so easy on the eyes."

"Hey, that's my wife you're talking about!"

"I don't mean no harm, Joe. I'm just saying that you and your wife got married right out of high school, right?"

"Yeah, we were high school sweethearts. She's been the only girl for me."

"Yeah, that's what I'm saying. She's been your only girl. You've got no one to compare her to. And don't even get me started on how boring life would be if all you ever got to eat was vanilla pudding, Joe. And there's a nice cream pie who's just standing there, looking at you, waiting to be tasted. I'm not saying to eat the whole pie, Joe. I'm just saying that you should take a taste of it – of her. What your wife doesn't know won't hurt her, right? Here, have another cocktail to help you get those pesky morals out of your way, Joe."

"Another drink? When did you order this?"

"Just a little while ago. Now that drink cost me five bucks, Joe. I expect you not to waste it. Oh, would you look here? She and her equally as tasty friend are heading our way. I tell you what, Joe. Just to make it easier for you, I'll take her friend. That way you won't be all alone in this. We'll both be doing it. No one will ever know, Joe. No one.

"I'll know."

"Not if I buy you a few more drinks, you won't."

What Would You Do

1. If you were in Joe's situation, what would you do?

2. If you were in Marsha's situation, what would you do?

3. If you were being persuaded to do something you wanted to do but knew that you shouldn't, what would you do?

Chapter 4
Never Buy a Pig in a Poke

Deception is something we have to deal with every day. The old pig in a poke saying refers to the idea that we shouldn't purchase something that we can't see for ourselves. Trusting what someone says about anything isn't always the best practice.

With buying so many things off the internet in recent times, I'm sure everyone has gotten something they didn't intend to get when making purchases off the world wide web.

Even when you buy something at the store that's packaged in a way that you can't see the contents has disappointed most of us at one time or another. With deception being such a huge part of life, what can we do, if anything, to avoid being duped? And how can we stop lying to ourselves?

When We Catch Ourselves Lying

I sat there, watching my coworkers coming into the building I was a security guard at. Being that the company was small, we all knew each other, and most of us got along well.

One by one, everyone trickled into the building to get to their respective offices. When I saw Jennie from accounting getting out of her car in the parking lot, I gasped. She'd not only dyed her hair. She'd gotten it cut too. One of those cuts where half of her head was shaved and the other half was all choppy. And the dye job was something out of a horror movie too – blues and reds and even purples.

For a moment, I had to run through my mind what day it was. April Fools? Halloween?

Nope.

Jennie came in, her lips pressed in a hard line as she looked nervous. "Hi, Amy"

"Hi, Jennie." I tried not to stare or let my mouth agape.

She ran her hand through the side of her hair where she still had some. "I went for a new look."

"I see that."

"It's been a thing I've wanted to do for a while now."

"It has?"

"Yeah. I'm going to audition for a music show next week."

"And you thought this would help?

"Yeah."

"Oh."

"So, what do you think about it?" She twirled around so I could see the back and I saw that a tic-tac-toe design had been shaved into her hair just above her backbone. "And be honest, please."

Now how in the world could I be honest with this woman?

"Since you're going to be auditioning for that music show, I think you must've done the right thing." *There, that's not too much of a lie.*

"But what do you think about it? Is it a good look for me?"

It's not a good look for anyone.

But I couldn't say that. "Um, yeah. It looks great. You really stand out now, Jennie."

"Thanks. That's exactly what I was going for."

"Well, you've accomplished it alright." So, I couldn't get out of lying to her, sue me!

When We Lie for a Good Reason

"Look, Mom, I know you and Dad never told us about the Easter Bunny or Santa Clause."

"Those are lies, and in our house, we don't tell lies, Sissy."

"I know. But Rob and I want Sam and Lola to get to have those little fantasies that all the other children their age are getting to have. It's not fair for our four-year-olds to be left out of the holidays just because you and Dad don't want to bend the truth a little."

"Bend it? You mean break it into smithereens, don't you? Or have you forgotten that those things don't exist at all and never have?"

"Mom, please, I really don't want to argue. You are to smile and just nod when the kids talk about the Easter Bunny or Santa. Got it?"

"No way. It's an out and out lie and I won't do it."

"Then I guess you can't ever see your grandchildren until they get too old to believe in those kinds of things. And just so you know, Sam lost a tooth earlier today and the tooth fairy will be paying him a visit tonight after he goes to sleep."

"Why are you doing this to us? All we ever did was be honest with you. What's the big deal? Why can't you just do the same things with your kids that we did with you and your brother?"

"Because my husband got to have Santa and all the rest of the mythical creatures and his childhood sounds like a dream come true to me, Mother! So, what's it going to be? See your grandkids now or wait until they're ten or so?"

"You win, you beast!"

"You mean, the kids win, Mom."

When Lies Sell

I took my sixteen-year-old son to buy his first car. He had five thousand dollars he'd worked hard for and he was ready to make the purchase. We'd come a long way to see a car that a man was selling from his home.

As we pulled up to the place, I had my doubts right away. "I knew it, Timmy. This place is a dump. There's no way this man has a car that's only four-years-old and in pristine condition for what you've got to pay. We should just go and not waste our time."

"Dad, please," Timmy begged with pleading eyes. "Can we just take a look at it?"

I didn't want to disappoint my son, but I knew this man wasn't going to be anything but a snake in the grass. "You'll see, son. Consider this a lesson in deceptive selling practices."

"Maybe it's not, Dad. The picture looked great. You saw it. That mustang looked like it was brand new."

"Yeah, and things in that kind of condition don't ever come so cheap. But you'll see."

We got out and headed to the front door. When a Pitbull came around the corner of the house only to be stopped by the chain he had on, we both came to a stop. "Whoa," Timmy said. "What a dog, huh, Dad?"

I knew there was something not on the up and up with this man and the dog just proved it that much more. "We really should go, son."

The front door opened, and there stood a short man, wearing shorts, no shirt and sunglasses. "Hey, you must me little Timmy who called about the Mustang. You ready to ride, homeboy?"

"I sure am." Timmy looked around. "Where's the car, Mr. Smith?"

He pointed out back to where a nearly falling down garage stood in the back of the house. "In there. You don't leave something like that out on the street. Let's go take a look at it."

"Can you drive it out here?" I asked as I took hold of my son's arm to stop him from running off after the man, we didn't know at all.

He stopped and looked at me with his head tilted to one side. "Um, no. This way, please."

I made Timmy stay back with me. We barely moved as we followed the man and I whispered, "I really think this is a terrible idea. We should just leave. I can say that I got a phone call and it's an emergency."

"No, Dad. Come on. You're acting like a chicken." Timmy rolled his eyes.

"I'm not a chicken. I'm just not stupid."

The man opened a door on one side of the garage. "Come on. It's in here."

"Why don't you open up the large garaged door?" I asked, warily. "We *will* want to take it for a test drive if he likes it."

"Oh? Well, I can't let you drive it. You can start it and if Timmy wants it, then he can drive it out of here. Once I have the cash in hand."

"Oh, great!" Timmy hurried to go inside the dark garage as I tried to keep up. His eyes were on the prize. "Oh, wow! Look, Dad. It's just like the picture. It's gorgeous!"

I had to admit. There was a car sitting in that dingy, ramshackle garage that matched the picture we'd seen on the texts the man had sent to Timmy. "It certainly looks like the same car."

"Oh, it is the same car," Mr. Smith told me. "It's ready to go too. I've got it all filled up with gas. That way you don't have to stop on your way out of town. You can just get in the car and drive all the way back to your home. Timmy said it was five hours away. Is that right?"

"Yes, that's right." I had the feeling something wasn't exactly right with the car. "And you only want five thousand dollars for this car? Can I ask why the low price? What's wrong with it?"

"Nothing is wrong with it." He ran his hand over the shiny black paint. "It's a beauty. And I just want to give this kid a great deal on his first car. He told me how hard he's worked for that money. Normally, I'd charge over ten thousand for a car this nice. But for Timmy, I seemed to have gotten a soft spot in my heart for him."

My son jumped into the driver's seat then got back out. "Um, where's the key?"

"Oh, we lost it. But you can use that screwdriver on the passenger seat to start it up. It runs great. Try it out." The man looked at me as he shrugged. "My wife, she's no good with small items. She lost them all the time. She lost the keys this morning."

"Dad, how do I do this?" my son called out as he attempted to understand how the screwdriver could start the car.

"Timmy, get out of the car, son." I looked at the man who was trying to sell my kid an obviously stolen car. "Look, you're not dealing with some idiot here. This is a stolen car. We'll be on our way."

Timmy was suddenly at my side. Clutching my arm as he pleaded, "No, Dad! Please. What's wrong? We can get another key. Please!"

"The car's not stolen," Mr. Smith assured me. "I swear."

"Dad, please!" Timmy cried. "This car is like a dream come true for me."

"I've got a deal for you, Timmy. If Mr. Smith has no problem with me giving the local police station a call to see if they can send an officer over here to run the VIN number and make sure this car isn't stolen first, then I'll let you buy it."

Mr. Smith went pale. "Um, see I don't get along with some of the officers on our local police force. But my cousin is a security guard. How about if he okays the car?"

Timmy broke into a smile. "Sounds good to me, Mr. Smith. I trust you one hundred percent."

"I don't. No cop, no car." I crossed my arms over my chest. "Do we have a deal?"

The man shook his head. "Sorry. No deal."

I took hold of my son's arm as he drags his feet. "Come on, Timmy. This isn't the car for you."

"But, Dad."

I leaned in close to whisper, "It's stolen, son."

"I don't even care," Timmy said.

"So, you would give this man your hard-earned money just to drive this car until the police found out it was stolen and came to take it from you to give back to the rightful owner?"

"What if they never found out?" Timmy winked at me. "I won't tell if you don't."

"Get your hind end into my car. We're going to have a very long talk on the five-hour trip home, boy!"

When Lies Hurt

"So, tell me why you said it then if you never meant it?"

"I'm sorry, I really am. I just felt like I had to say it. You'd said it, so I felt like I needed to say it back to you."

"Even though it was a lie? Didn't you think that I would figure out that you didn't really love me? Especially when I saw you with that other man?"

"I don't know what I was thinking. I never meant to hurt you."

"Well, it does hurt. You told me that you loved me. I believed you. I went and bought you an engagement ring. That's how much I believed you. I was ready to marry you."

"I didn't know that. I wouldn't have said yes to a marriage proposal."

"Sure. You'd just lie to me about loving me. I get it."

"I never meant to hurt you."

"It doesn't matter how many times you say that. It still hurts."

When Lies Make You Laugh

I came into the kitchen to find my three-year-old daughter with chocolate all over her face. "Della, did you get into the chocolate cake that I have in the refrigerator?"

"No, Mommy. You said not to, so I didn't get into it."

I opened the fridge to find the cake now on the bottom shelf and a whole handful had been taken out of it. "Well, did you happen to see who stuck their hand in the cake and who also moved it off the shelf I had it on?"

"Um," she swayed back and forth, oblivious to the chocolate cake left on her face and hands. "Maybe a robber did that."

"You think someone broke into our house and robbed us of a handful of chocolate cake?"

She nodded. "Uh, huh."

"I guess I should call the police."

"Yeah, you should cause that's not right to steal someone's cake."

"Can you describe the person who came in and took the cake?" I asked her as I took out my phone.

"Yes, I think it was a tall man with a mustache and some suspenders that looked like rainbows."

"Really?" I tried not to laugh. "And what should I tell the police about why you have chocolate cake on *your* face and hands? And what about those handprints on the fridge too? They're small, just like *your* hands are."

She looked at the chocolatey prints on the fridge she'd just seemed to notice. "Oh, those. Yeah, he had tiny hands too."

"And *your* face and hands?" I asked. "How did *they* get the stolen cake on them?"

"Well, Mommy. It was really sad. He threw the handful of cake at me. It hit me in the face, and I had to use my hands to wipe it off."

"So, this robber broke into our house, and he stole some cake. And he did that just so he could throw it at you?" I had to struggle to keep the smile off my face as she was dead serious.

She shrugged. "I guess he has some issues, Mommy."

That was it. I broke into laughter as she just stared at me like I was insane.

When Lies are Devastating

"So, where were you then, Joe?"

"I was at the bar. I told you that."

"I mean the rest of the night, Joe. You didn't spend the night at the bar."

"Look, I got drunk and slept in my car, okay? I didn't want to tell you that. I didn't want to admit to doing that. You were out of town on that business trip and I was out with the guys from work for the first time since I started working there. And one thing led to another and I had too much to drink.

You know I don't ever drink. I think I only had three or four, but they were too much for me."

"I came home early, Joe. I drove past the bar you said you were going to and there were no cars in the parking lot. I came home and you weren't here."

"Did I say I stayed in the parking lot? No, I did not. I drove a little way. They knew I was too drunk to drive. I pulled into an apartment complex that's not too far from the bar."

"And you want to tell me that you fell asleep in your car? You never got out of it? You never went into anyone's apartment to spend the night?"

"That's right. I fell asleep in my car and when I woke up it was light outside, so I started it and came home."

"You didn't know anyone who lived in that apartment complex, Joe? Not a woman named Natasha?"

"No. I don't know anyone named Natasha? I did what I said, and I don't appreciate getting treated like this."

"Like what, Joe?"

"Like a liar."

"See, here's the thing, Joe. Our marriage is on the line here. Do you realize that?"

"I don't see why it would be. I was out, had too much to drink, then slept in my car. There's nothing to divorce over."

"If you had done that, then you are right, there would be nothing to divorce over. But you're lying to me, Joe. To add to the humiliation and betrayal of what you've done to me, now you want to stand here and lie to my face."

"What makes you think that I'm lying to you? What makes you think that I would do anything to jeopardize our marriage?"

"My best friend lives next door to Natasha, Joe. When I got home and couldn't find you, I saw a text that I hadn't noticed that had come in from her earlier in the night. She asked me if I was aware that you and another man wearing a suit and tie just like you were visiting the girls who live next door to her. I was not aware of that. So, I called her up and guess what, Joe? She was still up. Want to know why?"

"Not really."

"Well, I'm going to tell you anyway. She was up because the noise from her next-door neighbors and their guests was so loud, she could not sleep. She told me I should come over."

"So, you went to her place last night after you got home?"

"I did. I went over to her place and I saw your car parked in front of Natasha's apartment, Joe. I looked in your car to make sure you weren't there. I used the key I have to it and unlocked it, opened it up so I could be sure you weren't in it anywhere, not even in the trunk. I wanted to be thorough, Joe."

"And you're sure that was *my* car?"

"My key worked on it. Yes, I am sure it was *your* car. Your blue suit jacket had been left on the passenger seat. Red lipstick stained the collar."

"I don't recall any of that."

"Do you recall a woman screaming your name in the throes of passion over and over, Joe?"

"I do not recall anything like that, no."

I had no choice. I picked up my cell phone, showed him the picture of his car, showed him the picture of him leaving the apartment in the sun's early morning light. And then I let him hear the recording I'd made. "Get out, Joe. Our marriage is over."

When We Have to Lie

My husband came to me one day after work. He looked worried, nervous, and very anxious. "You look awful. What's going on?"

"Where are the kids?"

"Playing with the neighbor kids next door. Why?"

"They can't hear what I've got to tell you. No one can."

I wasn't sure I wanted to hear what he had to say. "Although I'm probably going to regret hearing it, what is it?" I figured it couldn't be that bad.

"I had an accident today." He ran his hand over his face. "My car's totaled."

My heart raced. "What do you mean? How can that be? Why didn't you call me?"

"I couldn't call you. I didn't *need* to call you. It was taken care of."

"How?" I was lost.

"I'm not who I've said I am. And things have changed. We've got to move."

He was acting nuts, talking crazy. Maybe he'd hit his head in the accident or something. "I don't understand." I wasn't taking the kids and moving. I wasn't going to listen to his crazy talk.

He grabbed me by my arms, holding me tight. "I'm not able to stay here anymore. You and the kids have to come with me. It's a matter of life and death."

The doorbell rang and panic filled my husband's eyes. "Why do you look like that?"

"You can't tell anyone that I'm here. You haven't heard from me. Got it?"

"Why?

"There's no time to explain. You don't know where I am. If they ask you to call me, then do it. I won't answer and you will just stick to your story. You haven't heard from me since I left for work this morning."

"I won't lie to the police. If you hurt someone in that accident, then you have to face what you've done." I wasn't going to let him hide from what he'd done.

"It's not the police. It's the mafia. Now do as I've told you too, or they will kill me, then you, and then they will kill our children."

I couldn't believe him. I walked to the door as he went to hide in the cellar. Three men in black suits stood at my door. One of them asked, "Is your husband around?"

"No, I haven't heard from him since he left for work this morning."

Exercises in Morality

1. You hit a car in the parking lot of a large grocery store. No one saw you do it. You look around and there are no cameras. What do you do?

2. One night you're out with friends, drink a bit too much and end up kissing a coworker that your husband has always accused you of having a thing for. Do you tell him what you've done?

3. Your sister comes to see you. She's gained a lot of weight since you've seen her last. She tells you that you look great and asks how she looks. What do you say?

Chapter 5
Covert Take Overs

Covert hypnosis might sound like something that just wouldn't work. After all, a person has to be aware of things if they are going to be hypnotized. The back and forth action of an old pocket watch repeated words. You're getting sleepy. Those kinds of things can't be done without the subject knowing what you're trying to do.

Earlier we talked about NLP. Some of the people who practice this claim to be able to contact the unconscious mind of others. Manipulating thoughts of others without others being aware of what they are doing is what covert hypnosis is.

Of course, with something this sinister, there are huge controversies surrounding the subject. But I'm not here to debate things. I'm here to give you some ideas on how covert hypnosis could work.

Then you can decide if it's real or made up just to scare people.

Using Sleep Deprivation to get People to do What You Want

Who of us hasn't ever been sleep deprived? I know I have, and I know my brain felt like cold Jell-O inside my head. Whatever anyone told me I'd done, I simply agreed.

I'd spent a sleepless night with a sick baby. Just as I would doze off, there would go the crying again. I'd get up, walk with him, sit and rock with him, and nothing would work. So, I ended up in the living room, walking, rocking, and watching television just to try to keep my eyes open.

Morning came, everyone else got up and my husband came to me with the television remote in his hand. "Found this in the fridge next to the butter. Care to explain?"

"I didn't do it." I had no recollection of even going to the kitchen, much less carrying the remote and putting it in the fridge.

"No one else was up. You and little John were the only ones. I don't think our six-month-old did it." He laughed. "It's okay. You were out of it. Still are by the looks of things." He gestured to my bathrobe that hung off my nearly naked body. "I'll take him, and you go take a shower."

Glad to hand the baby over, I went to the shower and while under the hot water, I really tried to recall when I had put the remote in the fridge. I had no recollection what-so-ever of doing it.

My job as a detective had me thinking I might try this on some of my perps to get them to admit to things they'd done. So, I took on my first perp that next week.

He'd been brought in on suspicion of human trafficking. I really wanted to get him. So, I had him brought into an interrogation room. And there I let him sit for three hours. Every time he laid his head down, I had an officer go in and wake him up, telling him I was on my way and would be there soon.

Once I saw the signs of fatigue, the drooping eyes, the glazed look, the body that slumped and couldn't sit up straight no matter what, I went in. "Hi. Sorry for the wait."

"Yeah. It's been a while. And this wooden chair ain't all that comfy."

"Yes, I know. I apologize. I just had lots to take care of. So, I'll make this quick. You were found with some items, rope, zip-ties, duct tape, and even some chloroform."

"Yeah, me and my girlfriend like to get kinky."

"Is that so?"

"Yeah. So, can I go now?"

"Not yet." I tapped on the desk, nice and slow, repetitive. I watched out of the corner or my eye as his eyes got droopier and droopier. "What did you say your girlfriend's name was again?"

"Um, I think I said Rosa."

He hadn't even been asked that question. "Yeah, Rosa." I jotted that down, still tapping the desk in the same fashion. "And you bought that stuff we found in your trunk at the Fastbreak?"

"Um, if that's what I said, yeah."

"Did I ask you that?" I kept tapping.

"Didn't you?"

"Hmm, I can't recall. But you did buy that stuff at Fastbreak." I wrote that down. "At noon earlier today."

"Yeah." He looked down at the table. "Or no. No, I didn't do that. I didn't buy that stuff there. I bought it online."

I smiled, happy to have him telling me some truths. "No, you said you bought it at Fastbreak, I asked you about that when I first came in. Don't you remember that?"

"Oh, yeah. Sure."

Waiting a moment, I asked, "And you said your girlfriend is Sally?"

He nodded. "Yeah."

I had him right where I wanted him. "So that is Sally that was in the car with you when you were picked up?"

"Sure. Sally."

"And she was in, on the whole, playing Mr. Grey thing?"

"Yeah?"

"Then why did she run when the cops showed up?"

"I told her to."

"Why?"

"So, she wouldn't talk."

"And why didn't you want her to talk?"

"You know."

"Oh, yeah. Because of what you said earlier."

"What did I say earlier?"

"How she and you were looking for girls to add to your party. You know, as you said, you wanted to show them a good time too and how fun it is to pick up random women who don't know a thing. They're scared at first, but then they get into it and before they know it, they like doing it and it doesn't bother them at all that men pay you so they can do with them whatever they want."

"Yeah, and they get a room and food too. Like, they're winning, ya know?"

"Sure. They get a job and you get money too. A win-win, right?"

He nodded. "Sure. A win-win. I find them on the street or in a club and they get a new life. They love it."

"And you said you keep them at the Shady motel, right?"

"Did I say that?" He shook his head. "I'm beat. I messed up. I meant the Limelight motel."

I knew I had used some serious mind games on the man, and I knew we were about to find some missing girls and put this man away for a long time.

Playing on Old Fears to get People to do What You Want

I know this wasn't the right thing to do. I had come in late, knew the rules about my curfew, and knew I couldn't get grounded for the week. I had other things to do. Important things. So, I did what I had to do to stay out of trouble.

Curfew was two a.m. I was pulling into our driveway at four a.m., two hours late. My mother was already up, drinking coffee in the living room. She'd turned on the overhead light in the living room, and the porch light too. She was ready and waiting for me to arrive.

I knew I was in for it - and big time. So, what could I do to circumvent the consequences of my actions?

Lie?

Bring up ancient fears in my mother?

Win?

With it still being dark outside, I had that to my advantage. Unseen monsters could still be lurking around that my mother wouldn't be able to see. And with her active imagination and penchant for freaking out over the smallest of things, I used what I knew to my advantage.

Getting out of the car, racing to the front door, I rushed inside, closing the door behind me. "Oh, my God! Did you see it, Mom?"

With my frightened demeanor, my mother already looked a little worried. "What are you talking about? I didn't see anything. Do you know what time it is?"

"Mom, you didn't see that black dog? I think it might've been that stray lab that we saw a few days ago. Remember, it was lurking around in the brush down the street? Mom, it jumped out at the car when I drove by it. I didn't see it at first and nearly hit it. But I managed to miss it. But then it chased me. I'd slowed way down so I wouldn't hit it and that dog was biting at my taillights. Mom, it wouldn't stop barking and growling and biting at the car. And it wouldn't stop chasing me.

"Oh, Lord!" She jumped up and went to look out the window. "I don't see anything. Did it damage the car?"

"I don't really know for sure. It was biting at the bumper and the tires." I recalled an old story my mother had told me about seeing a dog with rabies when she was a kid. "Mom, I think it was foaming at the mouth."

"No!" She locked the door. "Maybe it has gotten rabies and gone mad."

"Yeah, that's what I was thinking." I went to get myself a bottle of water and acted like I was trying to calm down. "Man, that was really scary."

"Oh, I know. I'm shocked that you got out of the car." She kept looking out the window. "I just hope it hears something else and runs off. Dogs with rabies just go after the next thing making noise. It drives them nuts when they hear anything. That's why it bit at the car and wouldn't leave it alone. And had you made enough noise. It would've taken off after you."

"I was being as quiet as I could when I got out of the car. I made sure I didn't see it, but I think I heard it still biting at the bumper." I sat on the sofa, pulling the blanket off the back of it and propping my head on the armrest. "I better sleep in here with you, just in case you see it. I won't be able to rest if I think you might actually go out there and try to kill it."

"No, I'll call the police if I see it. They'll come to take care of it." She sat back down, picking up her coffee cup with shaking hands. "But I'd rather you be in here anyway. I heard a story once about a rabid dog who jumped through a window. The windows in your bedroom go almost all the way to the floor. You get some sleep. I'll keep a watch out for it. Poor dog. I feel terrible for it. It's in such pain right now."

"Yeah, it is. Night, Mom."

"Night, sweetie. You just rest now. I know how traumatic that must have been for you."

"Thanks, Mom. I love you."

Mission accomplished.

Using Panic to make People do What You Want

Case-study: The perp used panic to incite a mass evacuation from the Center for Performing Arts.

The night was calm. A string quartet played softly as the nearly filled stadium of people hummed along. The scene, one of serenity. So, what could possibly happen to get all of these people to scramble to anywhere but inside the safety of that building?

And more importantly, why would anybody want to do such a thing?

I had a lot of questions and no answers. But I was going to get to the bottom of things.

Thankfully, I had the woman who had pulled off the terrible feat in custody. She was tired and willing to talk, finally.

All of five feet tall, the small woman didn't look like someone who went around creating mass chaos on the regular. "So, tell me why you did it, Tiffany."

"He left me." She stared at the floor. "He'd told me I was nothing but a fly on the wall. Too quiet. Too small. Too useless."

"He? Who is he?"

The young, maybe thirtyish, plain woman, with hair cut in a pageboy fashion, wasn't much to look at. She did kind of fade into the woodwork – and it seemed that she designed her look to do just that. "He. My first boyfriend. When we first met, he said he liked how quiet I was. He said he was done with flamboyant women who caused big scenes. He liked me for who and what I was."

"But then he left you and said unkind things to you before he did that." I knew that could really hurt a person. But why go out and try to get others to hurt themselves? "How long ago did he leave you, Tiffany?"

"A month ago." Her red-rimmed eyes slowly came up to meet mine. "Yesterday, I saw him and his new girlfriend. I accidentally bumped into him at the park. She told me off."

"His new girlfriend told you off yesterday?" I could see how that would ignite a fire in anyone.

"She's like almost six feet tall. And really loud and obnoxious. She told me ugly things - things about my height. She called me a troll." She had to stop and sigh.

"Well, you know you're not a troll. You're a beautiful young woman, Tiffany." I always tried to make anyone I talked to feel better. "So, what you're telling me is that she upset you. She upset you so much that you felt you had to do something big. Is that right?"

Nodding, she went on, "She poked me in the shoulder, then pushed me down. And he just watched her do it to me. She told me I couldn't do a thing to her. She told me that the man I had once loved was done with me. He had her now and he was so happy. He'd been miserable with me, is what she said. And when I looked into his eyes, he nodded. Then he finally said something to me."

"And what was that?"

"He told me that I would never amount to anything and that no one would ever even know so much as my name. Well, they will now, won't they?"

"Yes, they will. Only because you're going to go to prison for what you did, Tiffany."

"So." Her eyes went back to the floor. "I don't care. At least those two will have to see my face on the television. They will hear my name. Everyone will."

I had one more thing I had to know. "Tiffany, seeing as you've confessed to this crime. I'd like it if you would tell me how you got all of those people to run out of that building."

"Easy." A slight smile curled her lips. "I started that panic with one word. Bomb. I was in the bathroom, and there were other women in there too. I came out of the stall, acting freaked out and pointed at the empty stall as if something were really in it. Then I shouted with panic in my voice, 'Bomb!' They all ran, screaming, shouting the word, bomb, over and over again. I made them all say the same word. I made them all run. *I* did that. *Me*. Little, old *me*. See, I can make things happen when I really want to, can't I?"

Using Threats to get People to do What You Want

"Dolly, can you run to the bank for me? I need this check deposited this afternoon and I won't be able to take off from work until after lunch."

"Sure." I got up from my desk and went to get the check from my coworker. "While I'm out, you want a coffee?"

"That would be awesome. You're a doll, Dolly."

Nancy always said that little phrase. "Thank you." I never got tired of hearing it either. I liked to be of help to others.

I'd had a tough childhood. My parents had died in a car crash when I was ten. There were no relatives to take me in, so I was put into foster care. Passed from one family to another, I felt left out a lot. And I had to put up with being picked on most of the time too.

Now that I was grown, living on my own, I made it my goal in life to help others to try to put a good spin on my bad past. I'd said to myself that I wouldn't let all that negative rub off on me. I would show the world that one could go through adversity when young and still come out without being broken.

The bank wasn't too far from the building I worked as an administrative assistant in. I walked the five blocks to put my coworker's check in the bank. The company I worked for used the same bank as my coworker did. Making weekly deposits for my employer had me knowing pretty much all of the bank tellers by name and they knew mine too.

The bank was busy, as it was a Friday. I got in line at the back and waited patiently. When the door opened only a few seconds later, I felt a chill run through me. Then a man came up behind me – way too close. I tried to take a step forward to give us more space, but I found him grabbing my arm, then felt something against my back.

His words came out quietly near my ear, "Just be calm and quiet and you won't get hurt."

Panic filled me, but the thing I instinctively knew was that a gun was pressed against my back and I wasn't going to do anything to get myself shot. "I'll do anything you want, just please don't hurt me or anyone else."

"Don't worry. As long as you do as I say, I won't hurt you or anyone else. But you've got to do everything I tell you to, or I won't only kill you. "He jerked his head at a little girl who was sitting in the common area alone, waiting on one of her parents to get through with their banking business." I'll kill that little girl too."

My heart stopped. "No." I knew he must have something horrible he wanted me to do.

"Yes." He slipped something into my hand. "Give the teller this note when they call you up. I'm going to be right there, sitting right across from that little girl while you take care of my business for me. There's a girl sitting in a black Mustang at the far-left corner of the bank. You take what the teller gives you and toss it into the passenger window of that car. It will be rolled down. From there, you take off, running through the back parking lot."

"They know me here."

"That doesn't matter to me at all. You just do what I say, and everyone will leave here alive. If you don't, then even if I miss hitting you, I *will* hit that little girl."

I was next in line as he left me, going to take a seat right across from that little girl. My mind raced with what else I could do besides rob the bank. I wasn't sure if I would go to jail over that or not. I knew if anything happened to that little girl, I would most likely want to kill myself.

My turn came. Annette smiled at me. "Hi, Dolly. How can I help you today?"

I held the paper in one hand and the check to deposit in the other. "Um, I've got a check to deposit." I slid the check and the deposit slip to her then waited as she did the transaction.

"It's nice outside today. Did you walk over?" she asked.

"I did walk over." I cut my eyes to find the little girl was still there, playing on a cellphone, unaware that the man who sat only four feet away from her could kill her at any second.

"Well, that's it. Here's the receipt, Dolly."

I took it, put it in my pocket then breathed in nice and deep. "I've got this for you too, Annette." I put the note on the counter.

She looked at it, then slipped it under her computer. "Oh, I see. Okay. Let me handle that for you." I watched as she hit the panic button just underneath the counter. "Are hundreds fine, Dolly?"

"Yes." I hadn't read the note. I had no idea what amount of money I was robbing from that bank. All I knew was that I was saving a life."

"I'll put this in an envelope for you, Dolly." Annette looked at me, dipping her head to get me to look at her. "Fifty-thousand dollars? That's right?"

I nodded. "Yes."

She smiled. "Dolly, it's going to be okay." She barely cut her eyes to the man who sat in the common area. "Do what you were told to do. Everything's going to be okay."

I nodded as I took the money then tried not to run out of the bank in a panic. I saw the car he'd told me about and went as calmly as I could to it, then tossed the envelope full of hundreds into the open passenger window. The woman driving, backed out then drove off.

I didn't run, I waited, hiding in the bushes near the place I knew the man would walk out. When he came out, I stopped breathing as he got into another car then drove away.

I wasn't leaving, didn't want to. I would wait for the police. A moment later, the little girl and her mother came out. I finally left my hiding place in the bushes. "Excuse me," I said.

The mother stopped as the child kept walking to the car. "I did it for her. If anyone asks you. If anything happens to me. I did it so your daughter wouldn't be shot."

"What?" she looked confused. The sounds of sirens came floating on the summer breeze.

"I did it for her. I robbed the bank for her."

"Get into the car, Jackie," the woman screamed.

The police cars came screeching into the parking lot. One of them was going so fast. They couldn't stop in time. The little girl was in the middle of the parking lot. "No!"

I stumbled back. My mind numb – I couldn't take it all in. "I did it for her! All for her! Why?"

The girl's mother rushed to her daughter, but it was too late. The police car had run right over her – the officer had never seen her as he was looking directly at me.

One day later, I couldn't take it anymore. That's why I left this note, to let everyone know why I robbed that bank and why I took my own life, twenty-four hours later.

Using Confusion to get People to do What You Want

As I sat in the back of the police car, a warm blanket wrapped around me, I knew I would be okay now. It was all over.

An officer got into the front seat, closing the door. "It's cold out there. We'll be out of here soon. Don't worry. We've got him. And the rest of the girls too."

"Good." I pulled the blanket around my scantily clad body a bit tighter. "My family must be worried sick about me. I've lost track of time. I don't know how long he had me."

"Your parents came in to tell the police that you had been missing since April second. That's eight months, Stacy."

"Wow." Eight months had passed, and I was barely aware of that.

"How'd he do it, Stacy?" the cop asked me. "How'd he get you to go with him?"

It didn't seem real that I fell for it all. But I had. "I was walking out of a grocery store. It was about nine at night. I'd picked up a frozen pizza to make at home. My shift had just gotten over. I worked there."

"Yeah, we know you worked at the grocery store. We know that a man came up to you and you two talked. Then you went with the man." He shook his head as if he couldn't believe it. "Why would you go with a strange man, Stacy? Your parents said it's not like you at all to go off with strangers."

"He was convincing." I shook as I recalled the exact words.

"Hey, lady. You work here?" a man asked me as I came out of the grocery store, I worked at.

"Yes, I work here. What can I help you with?" Even off the clock, I was still an employee at heart.

"I'm having trouble with my car," he said.

"Oh, I'll go back inside and ask one of the guys to help you out. I don't know a thing about cars. Sorry." I stopped to go back inside to see if I could get some man to help the guy.

"That would be awesome." He reached out and touched my arm, halting my actions. "But I've got this baby girl with me and she's crying like crazy too. My wife, her momma, is back home and I don't know what to do. Maybe you could sit in the car with her while I go inside and find another guy to help me out. Do you think you could that for me?"

Something told me not to do it. I felt a rush of cold move through my body. "Oh, I'm not sure."

All of a sudden, the man's cell phone went off. "Shit!" The ringtone was kind of odd, chaotic, and loud. I froze as he took the phone out of his pocket. "Honey, I'm trying to hurry." I could hear someone crying on the other end of the line. "Baby, I know you're sick. I'm trying to get the medicine. I'll be back as soon as I can. The damn car broke down on me." More crying and shouting on the other end of the line, then he said, "I'm sorry! I'm trying! I just need help."

"I'll go sit with the baby," I offered as the man seemed to be on the verge of tears and the woman on the phone was already in tears. I had no idea what was going on in their lives, but it sounded tragic. "Show me where the car is."

"Thank you. You're an angel sent from above." He walked toward the back of the parking lot and I walked along beside him. "Honey, this nice lady is helping now. I'm sure we'll be home soon. Try to rest until we get there. I love you, babe." He ended the call and put the phone back into his jeans pocket.

"Wow, it sounds like you all are having a really hard time." I saw the hood open on the one car parked in the back row. "What's wrong with the car? It just won't start or what?"

"Yeah, it won't start is all." He stopped at the back of the car. "Thanks a lot. We are having a really hard time. You can get into the back seat there. Little Lila is in her car seat. It's quiet. Sounds like she might've fallen asleep, thank the lord above. If you'll just get in and sit there in case she wakes up. I'll run back in and get some help."

"Sure. No problem at all." I opened the back passenger side door and saw an infant's car seat on the other side of the car. A baby, or what looked like one in the dark, was all bundled up inside of it. I got in, closing the door behind me to keep the cool night air out.

When the hood slammed shut, I jerked my head up to find the man had closed it and was getting inside the car, behind the wheel. I had no idea what was going on and tried to open my door, but it wouldn't open. I jumped over the baby and tried to open that door, but it wouldn't open either. "Stop! Let me out!"

The soft blankets where the baby should've been smelled weird. I pushed the blankets and found nothing was in them and the man wasn't speeding away but driving a normal speed to be leaving the parking lot. "Just go to sleep," the man told me.

My eyes were getting heavy and I had no idea why that was. "No. Let me out." I tried to climb over the seat to get out the front passenger door.

He pushed a rag against my face. "Just go to sleep."

I felt it all going black and fell back into the back seat. And that's all I remember about that. When I woke up, I was in a dark room, like a motel room and my clothes were gone, my hands and feet tied to bedposts.

I looked out the window of the squad car, watching another officer take the man who'd lied to me so convincingly and put him in the back of another cop car. "You know, I think I wouldn't have fallen for it if it wasn't for that damn phone call he got. It became so chaotic that I stopped thinking and just tried to solve the problem anyway I could."

"Yeah," the officer said. "He pulled covert hypnosis on you. He did it to most all the girls he kidnapped. He used chaos to get you out of your own mind. Then he put into your unconscious mind the need for help and you had no real choice except to help the man. It's a human reaction and he used it against you. It's a pretty damn dark and insidious way to get people to do what you want them to. I wish I could tell you that it would never happen to you again, but I'd be lying. It's actually been proven to work over an over again on the same people."

"No way!"

Let's See What You Think

1. You've read about some pretty dark ways to get people to do what you want them too. Would you stoop to using any of these tactics? And why or why not?

2. A woman comes up to you, crying inconsolably. She keeps trying to get you to come with her, but you're not sure why. It seems important though and she seems so upset that she couldn't actually harm you. Do you go with her to help or do you walk away? Why or why not?

3. You've got a lot on your plate at work. Your boss has given you a strict timeline to get a project done. You will not be able to get it done on time and he's told you that your job is on the line. Do you come up with an

elaborate tale to get your boss off your back and get your time extended? Or do you accept the fate of being fired?

Chapter 6
Hostile Mind Takeover

Brainwashing – a scary word. No one wants to believe that they could be brainwashed, but it happens. It happens more than you even know.

Brainwashing is known by other names too – mind abuse, coercive persuasion, and thought control. What happens, is a person or even a group of people use systematic methods to get the victim to bend or conform to things they wouldn't conform to otherwise. Think about members of a cult.

That's scary, but even scarier is the fact that advertisers have learned these dark techniques and use them regularly on the unsuspecting public.

To make this complex subject easier to understand, I've written some life-like scenarios for you.

Only One Conclusion

The day was long, the food supply limited, and picky eaters would prove hard to deal with. I was alone with my two sons in a remote cabin in the woods. Their father had gone out hunting and wouldn't be back for at least two days.

We were on our own with the little we had. My ten and twelve-year-old sons didn't care for much, other than fast food. I had my work cut out for me.

Not young enough to force them to eat what I wanted them to, the boys would have to *want* the food I had to offer.

But how to get pre-teens to think they actually wanted to eat something they'd turned down most of their lives?

"Hey, I was reading the other day how the turkey is a superfood." I brought up.

"Turkey?" Garrett asked as he made a face. My twelve-year-old thought himself a connoisseur of not so fine foods. "If that's such a superfood, then why isn't it sold at any of the places we eat, Mom?"

"Well, grapes are a superfood and you can't get them at the places you eat either." I felt that needed to be pointed out. "And we are out here in the wilderness - twenty miles from any town. If your dad doesn't make it back for any reason, then we'll have to hoof it out of here. And the snow is only getting deeper by the day."

"Are you saying that we should build ourselves up in case we have to walk out of here, Mom?" Bryan, our ten-year-old asked.

I shrugged. "You never know. Might as well be prepared, right?"

My sons looked at each other then Garrett asked, "So, what about this turkey you read about?"

"It's a superfood. It's got protein and other vital nutrients."

"Yeah, and it's gross," Bryan said.

"Do you think that muscle building protein is gross, Bryan?" I asked.

Garret flexed his tiny bicep. "I'm strong enough."

"Are you?" I looked out the window as the snow fell outside of it. "Are you strong enough to fend off, let's say, a wolfpack?"

Both boys looked a little on the frightened side. "Nope," they said.

"Do you think that eating a superfood, like a turkey could help you fight them off if it came to it?" I asked.

Bryan nodded. "Superfood is in the name, so I would think it could help."

"And what about hunger? Walking all that way, twenty miles could deplete your energy. My bets are on that it would. Wouldn't it be best to have fueled your body with the best stuff you could so that you would have stamina much longer than if you'd eaten junk?"

Garret agreed, "Yeah, eating superfoods sounds like the best thing to do if you're faced with something like that."

"Yeah," Bryan agreed.

"So, if you had the choice to eat cheese pizza or a turkey sandwich on whole grain bread, which would you pick if you had to walk twenty miles in the snow and possibly take on a pack of wolves along the way?"

"Turkey sandwiches!" they both shouted.

"Great." I got up to go make them some. "Since we have no idea what we're in for. Do you boys think tonight's dinner should be some turkey sandwiches or that one frozen cheese pizza we've got?"

"Turkey sandwiches!" they shouted again.

And we have a winner!

The Same Phrase

"My mother had a new friend over the other day and something she said just won't leave my mind," I told my husband. "And Mom has been going to meet with this little church group with this woman for over a week. Now, Mom's saying this thing a lot and I don't know if I like it."

"What is it?" he asked me.

"It seems benign. I know it does, but it's just that her friend said it over and over. And now Mom's doing it." I couldn't shake the feeling that something bad might happen if I didn't tell someone what I'd overheard.

"So, what is it, Beth?" my husband asked, growing impatient.

"The name of the man who heads up this little church group – a group who meets in the member's homes, instead of a real church – is Barney." Even saying his name gave me chills.

"And what does that have to do with what this woman and your mother have been saying?" he asked me, looking aggravated as he rubbed his temples.

"It's his name. The woman kept starting out her sentences with, Barney says. It was odd. She said things like Barney says we should all eat tuna fish. My mother asked her why and I swear to you that the woman merely shrugged and said that she didn't know. No one asks Barney why he says the things he says – that would be rude. Anyway, she went on to say that since she's added tuna to her diet, she feels great."

"That's not so bad," my husband said as he laid back in our bed. "I don't see what you're worried about."

"She said other things too. Like this, Barney said we all need to put ten dollars into the pot each time we meet. And she also said Barney, says we need to meet every other day, so we don't forget the words." I shrugged. "I don't know what she meant by that, but I didn't like it. And I didn't like what I found at Mom's today."

"What did you find at your mother's house?"

"A whole shelf in her pantry is nothing but canned tuna fish. And she's got an envelope from her bank with nothing but ten-dollar bills in it too." I just knew something wasn't right with this little church group. "And she told me that she joined that group and then she said this, Barney says we should all bring at least one new person to our group each month. Barney says when we get one hundred followers that we can buy a place where we all can live. Like a camp. We will all live in one, great big home, and we will all take care of each other for the rest of our lives."

"Great!" my husband said. "I've always worried that your mother would end up living out the remainder of her years with us. Thank goodness she found this group."

"No! I think he's a cult leader or something." I smacked him on the arm. "She said that Barney says they are all going to put all their money into one account that he'll oversee and make sure everyone is taken care of."

"I still don't see a downside," my husband said, then snuggled down and went to sleep.

Too Many Questions

"How would you like it if a man took your wallet, Joey?" he asked me.

"I," I couldn't say anything else as he jumped right back in.

"How would you like it if someone stole your dog, Joey? How would you like it if you stepped on a nail? How would you like it if your mom went to jail? How would you like it if I took your stuffed teddy bear? How would you like it if you couldn't ever drink water again?"

"Stop!" I screamed.

But he didn't stop. "How would you like it if popcorn were no longer available? How would you like it if there wasn't any more snow, Joey? How would you like it if I ran over your toe with my car?"

"I wouldn't like any of those things."

"So, how would you like to go to the movies with me?"

"Movies? Yeah, sure." I hadn't wanted to go anywhere with him, but I'd do anything to shut him up.

When Fear Bends Your Mind

I sat at my desk in my office on the fifth floor when a strange man ran into my office, breathing hard and looking scared to death. "Thank God, I made it." He slammed the door closed behind him, locking it. "There's a fire out there. The whole place is on fire. I'm looking for all the survivors I can find to help them." He came at me quickly, pulling me out of my chair. "You've got to get out of here."

"I don't smell any fire."

"No, it's not quite here yet. But it's coming and it's coming fast. You're going to have to jump."

"I'm on the fifth floor! I can't jump."

"You would rather burn alive?"

"I would *not* rather burn alive."

He pushed me to the window then opened it. The ground looked so far away. "Here you go then, time to jump."

"But," I got up on the ledge. "I don't see any smoke."

"It's billowing out the other side. Hurry, there's no time to waste." He gave me a slight push. "Jump! Now!"

And so, I did and that was when I broke my legs all because of one crazy as sin man.

When Anger Bends Your Mind

"I said no!" she screamed at me.

I hadn't even wanted to drink the beer until she did that. "You aren't the boss of me."

"You will not drink that beer!"

"Um, hell yes I will. You won't tell me what I can and can't do. I am an adult."

"I will make your life a living hell if you drink even one sip of that beer!"

I turned it up and drank it all down. "To hell with you. I do what I want!"

Isolation and Brainwashing

Joe grew up on a remote farm with only his grandparents around. With only the three of them, Joe knew nothing more than what he'd been told his entire life.

When I got out of the car to pick him up and take him with me to a new home, a place where he'd be safe since the death of his grandparents, he tried to run away. "No. I won't go. You're not real!"

I had another caseworker come in from behind the small house. "It's okay. We're here to help you, Joe."

"No!" the fifteen-year-old boy screamed. "There's no one else on this planet. Why would they lie to me? Why?"

Joe was the victim of grandparents who thought it best to keep the boy unaware of outside life. They'd had to raise him from an infant when his mother took off and left him at their home. She was in a cult and they wouldn't let her keep the baby she'd been pregnant with before she joined them.

I had to try to make him understand why people he loved would do such a horrible thing to him, "They did it only because they loved you, Joe. But it was all a lie. Now come with us and everything will be okay. I promise."

He fell to his knees in the dark dirt. "They promised me too, lady. They promised me too!"

Brainwashing in Advertising

I sat there, my toothbrush in hand and the tube of toothpaste that I'd used for years and years in the other. "Nine out of ten dentists recommend this brand, Danny. You should use it too."

"How do you know that's true?" My new boyfriend came to stand at my side. "I use the other brand and guess what?"

"What?" I asked as I began brushing my teeth.

"That commercial says that nine out of ten dentists recommend my brand too. Think you might've been brainwashed?"

Have I?

Some Thought-Provoking Questions

1. For years you've been told that there is no snow on Mount Olympus. Then you see a picture of the mountain on television and see snow on it. How do you feel about that?

2. You go to a meeting with a friend and find the charismatic leader of her group has lots of ideas that are way out of the norm, but he's so cute and he's smiling at you so much. What would you do if he asks you to join the group and leave your family behind?

3. You find a man running into your workplace, screaming that terrorists are coming. You all have to hide. What do you do?

Chapter 7
Playing Games

The art of playing mind games has been practiced throughout history. Here are a few life-like scenes to help you spot them and hopefully help you to know when someone is playing with your mind.

Testing Your Faithfulness

"So, I'm seeing Joey, right," I told my best friend. "And he does this thing last night that totally freaks me out, but like in a good way, I guess."

"What did he do?"

"Well, his best friend called me all late and stuff and he asked me if he could come over. He told me that he really likes me and that Joey never had to find out."

"What did you do?"

"I totally told him that I was with Joey and that he needed to respect his friend a lot more than he was. And then I hung up on him."

"But how was Joey a part of that?"

"Oh, he called me right after and told me that he'd set me up. He gave me a test on faithfulness, and I'd passed. Yeah, me!"

"I think that was a pretty manipulative thing to do. You don't see it that way?"

"No way. It means he loves me."

"Not."

When They Really Want What You Have

"So, girl, I know you're in love and all that, but I saw your man, Tyrone, talking to Sara. Sara from the bar!"

"No way." I felt myself dying inside. "I thought he loved me."

"Yeah, I know right?"

"I don't know what to do."

"Break up with him before he gives you a disease, girl. You know what you got to do. Don't even tell him that you know about what he did. Just tell him that you don't love him anymore. Stick it to him before he can stick it to you."

"You're right. You're a great friend. Thanks, Ruth."

One week later...

Going into the club, I see Ruth sitting on Tyrone's lap. And by the look I found on her face, I think I had been played.

Getting Played Over Food

I sat down at the table in the cafeteria with my plate, hungry and ready to eat. "Boy, I am starving today."

Jane looks at my plate. She has nothing in front of her. "Yuck. That looks nasty. I bet they put dog food in that. That is what it looks like."

"It's chili." I look at the plate full of the food I had thought looked delicious.

"Well, chili or not, it looks like it came out of a can with a dog's face on it." She turns her nose up and looks the other way.

No longer looking at the food the same way, I feel my stomach rumbling for something else. "I'm gonna go get a bag of chips. This does look disgusting." When I come back, the plate is empty. "Um, who ate that nasty stuff, Jane?"

"I did." She wiped her mouth off. "Turned out. It was good after all."

And I ate my stale chips as I kicked myself for falling for that load of bull.

Played for Money

"Momma! Momma!" I walked into the house to see if I could score some cash to go to the movies.

"What?" she called out.

"Momma, I need some money."

"Nope."

I found her on the sofa, watching television. "Please."

"No. You still haven't done the yard work I asked you to do last week. I gave you ten dollars for that before you did the work. I ain't falling for that ploy again."

"All I need is five bucks, Mom. Look, if you give me the five, then I'll not only do the yard work, but I'll sweep and mop the whole house for you tomorrow."

"I don't know. I can't trust you."

"Sure, you can. I promise."

"Well, I guess I can give you one more chance." She takes out a five and gives it to me. "Have fun tonight. Tomorrow though, you got to work."

The next day…

I'm hurrying out the door. "Hey, where are you going? You promised me you'd do the yard and sweep and mop, remember?" Mom asked.

"Aw, man. I forgot that I've got a basketball game, Momma. Sorry, the team needs me. You understand, right? Love you. Got to jet."

I'd had my fingers crossed behind my back when I made that promise anyway!

Played for a Fool

I saw this ad in the paper for a boxer puppy for free and went to see if I could get it. When I came up to the house, I saw an old man sitting on the porch. "Mister, I'm here for that boxer puppy you've got for free."

"Oh, good. I've been needing a good home for my puppy." He got up and went inside then came out with a tiny dog that looked nothing like a boxer. "Here he is."

"Um, it's pretty small." I took the puppy out of his hands.

"He's only six weeks old."

"The ad said you've got papers for him. It said he was registered."

"Oh yeah, I forgot. Let me go get them." He came back with a piece of paper. "Here you go."

The paper looked legit. "You got pics of his parents?"

"Sure do." He pulled out his phone and showed me many photos. "See?"

Nodding, I left with my free registered boxer puppy.

A few months later, when my dog hadn't grown even a little, I took it to the vet to see what was wrong with it. Turned out nothing was wrong with my puppy. It was a full grown chihuahua was all.

Seemed I'd been played for a fool.

What Would You Do

1. You've got to get rid of some kittens. You have to move, and you need them gone to good homes fast. They all have these cool stripes that look a lot like those on a Bobcat. Do you advertise them as a rare breed of cats called, Manx's and maybe even make a buck or two from them?

2. You want to know if your girl is cheating, so you set her up to see if she'll fall for your friend. Do you feel this is right or wrong? And why?

3. You're starving but you have no money. Your friend has food that you'd love to eat. Do you make it seem unappetizing, so she won't eat?

Conclusion

Now some of the things you read in this book were funny and some were sad, while others where scary. All of them played on your emotions. They were meant to make you think.

Life isn't easy, fair, or even right at times. Sometimes it seems there is nothing we can do about it either. But that's not completely true. *You* can make a difference.

It's up to you what you do with what you've learned in this book. My hope is that you don't do anything you've learned in a bad way. But I do hope you learn to recognize when someonc is pulling some of this dark stuff on you or someone you care about. You've got the power to turn things around.

Life is unfair, tragic, and full of surprises. What you do with it is all up to you. Make your life count – for the good.

The End

Finally, if you enjoyed this book, then I'd like to ask you for a favor. Would you be kind enough to leave a review for this book on Amazon?

It'd be greatly appreciated!

Thank you and good luck!

Dark Psychology Judo

How to spot red flags and defend against covert manipulation, emotional exploitation, deception, hypnosis, brainwashing and mind games from toxic people –

Including DIY self-defense techniques

By Patrick Lightman

Introduction

No matter your age or where you live, you will experience deception. You will be on both ends of this darkness. You will do things you didn't think you'd ever do and things will be done to you that you never thought anyone would do. Even the people you love and trust the most in this world will deceive you more than once in your lifetime - and you will do the same to them.

What can you do about it?

How can you stop it from happening to you?

The answer to that is a simple one. You can't stop deception, manipulation, or even brainwashing from happening to you.

What can you do?

Learn to recognize these things and put a stop to them before they adversely affect you. You can learn how to circumvent the manipulators, liars, and brainwashers before they get a chance to embed themselves into your mind.

Within this book, you can learn the secrets to keep your mind safe and at ease. Along the way, you will learn how to stop yourself from doing these less than Heavenly acts too.

We all commit these types of dark psychology. Not even one of us is entirely innocent. Learn how to stop yourself from using the dark powers to your benefit and use the good ones to get what you want, instead.

It can be done. You can do this!

Darkness is all around us; there's no stopping it. But there are ways to see it, and to shed light on it, to lessen its strength. The worst that can happen is the dealer of these forces will leave you alone. The best that will happen is you will not be looked at as a victim any longer by the person using dark psychology to try to bend you to their will. They will see you as a person to be respected and no longer waste their time trying to get you to fall for their shenanigans.

Learning to stop using your powers of darkness will gain you respect as well. Being a trustworthy person also has its benefits. When people know they can take you at face-value, you earn their respect and trust. Those things go a long way in this world.

With this book, you will gain two valuable things. You will be able to see through people who use dark psychology to get people to do what they want them to. You will also gain the ability to stop yourself from using dark psychology to get what you want.

It's a win-win!

So, grab your beverage of choice – don't forget your favorite blanket – then cozy up in a comfy seat and get ready to fall into the pit of darkness, only to come out shining bright and thinking more clearly than you've ever thought before.

The journey is yours; all you've got to do is take it.

Chapter 1
Welcome to the Dojo

Chapter 1.1. The Basics of Dark Psychology Judo

As horrible as it sounds, everyone uses Dark Psychology. We're used to it. We see it in our government. We see it in our religions. We see it in our places of learning. We even see it at home. It's everywhere.

As daunting as that sounds, there are some things we can do about this apparent travesty of justice. They are seeing through the manipulators and the liars. The brainwashers are the biggest weapon a person can have in their possession.

One would think it would be easy as pie to see through someone using manipulations to affect them. One would be wrong.

Something as innocent as getting a child to pick up their toys with the enticement of a reward after the chore is considered to be a manipulation. You are using something against the child in order to get the desired response from them after all. Pick up the toys – get a prize. Don't, and you will get nothing.

The use of dark psychology has its place in this world, like it or not. It's used to train children to become competent adults. When it's used to try to train other adults to get them to do what you want out of them, then it becomes a problem.

When romantic partners use these dark tactics to get the other partner to bend to their will, it's not a very nice thing to do. When a boss uses these techniques to get what they want out of their workers, it's not a very nice thing to do. When people with deranged minds and agendas use dark psychology to get people to do what they want, it can be downright dangerous.

Knowing when someone is playing you, using you, or manipulating you will help you combat the darkness. Knowing is the best weapon there is. Ignorance can be dangerous.

Chapter 1.2. Know Your Opponent

Some people are more likely to misuse dark psychology. Personality traits, such as narcissism, machiavellianism, and psychopathy are huge red flags in general. People with these traits tend to use darker manipulation techniques than those without the traits.

The dark triad is a term that psychologists, law enforcers, and even business managers are sure to know. The dark triad refers to those three traits mentioned above. Knowing what type of person you're dealing with is essential in how you handle them.

Professionals need to know beforehand the types of tactics people with these traits will use to undermine them. They have to know what to look for, what to avoid, and how to combat the things these people will do.

A narcissist doesn't have much – if any – empathy for others – this includes animals. They think they're smarter than everyone else. Bloated egos, stern opinions, and a general lack of compassion go along with narcissism.

They want people to think they're more than what they really are. The outward appearance is important to them. People need to think everything is above par with them and their family. They want their world to be considered perfect by outsiders. They love to be envied and strive for it.

Narcissists are harsh judges, judging people harder than they judge themselves. As a matter of fact, they don't judge themselves. It's hard to judge one's self when one refuses to self-reflect. Looking outward at everyone else gives no time to look inward to see anything about themselves that might need working on.

You can spot a narcissist from a mile away – they make sure of it. They want to be the center of attention at any gathering; they refuse to sit back and be quiet. In their opinion, what they have to say is so much more important than what anyone else has to say, feel, or think.

Machiavellianism is quite the opposite of narcissism. This term is named after the man who embodied this trait – Niccolò Machiavelli. Born in 1469, this Renaissance period Italian became a diplomat and writer. As noble as that sounds, the man was anything but that.

He wrote a book about being a prince. In this book, he put his beliefs down for all the world to read. Immorality and brutality weren't wrong in his eyes. As a matter of fact, a person in power should use anything they have to, in order to win. And subjects should be treated harshly by their rulers, in his opinion.

In the seventies, a couple of psychologists made up a scale using the man's name to assess a person's personality. The Mach-IV test is used to gauge how many of traits of this personality disorder a person has, and it can be used to determine if they should be labeled with this disorder or not.

People with this dark trait come off most of the time as charming and have an inner confidence that makes people feel confident in them. The person with this disorder needs to pull people in so that they can use them to get what they want. They can't get it alone.

As charming as they can be, they're hard to get to really know. And if you did get to know them, a sane person wouldn't stay around them long. They use people, stooping to the lowest levels to do it. Nothing is out of bounds with these people. They can be some of the most dangerous people you will ever meet.

They too lack empathy. What hurts you, mentally or physically, doesn't matter to them. People who have these traits have been known to use torture to get people to do what they want.

People with Psychopathy show no remorse for their actions. Selfish, antisocial, and overall real jerks, these people don't think of others much at all.

Making impulsive decisions, it doesn't matter what the outcome is. With no remorse, things are much easier for them to do, even terrible things that inflict harm, both mentally and physically on others.

Now that you're armed with information on the three personality traits considered by experts as the worst of the worst, you have an edge most don't. You know what to look for when dealing with difficult people. And now you know when and whom you need to just walk away from.

These people can't change, no matter how much you think you can help them, you can't. As harsh as that sounds, it's the truth. You will only hurt yourself if you try to fix people with these traits. They have no desire to change themselves. It's quite the opposite; they only desire to change you, to make you do what will benefit them. If all they do is break you, or make you do something terrible, they're happy to have accomplished that feat.

Chapter 1.3. Know Yourself First

All of us have been brainwashed, manipulated, and lied to a bit by our parents and society. As humans, we're hardwired to take in information and use it as a basis to live by. It's what is expected out of us if we want to live with other people.

Some of the things we've been told are lies meant to keep us safe, so we won't wander off and get ourselves into danger. The bogey man was made up to keep us in our beds at night, instead of wandering all over the house while our parents slept.

Santa Clause, The Easter Rabbit, and other folklore were made up to get children to act good all year long. Be good, or Santa won't come.

Another lie our parents told us was not to make faces, or it will stick that way. I suppose this one was because they didn't want to see their kids looking crazy. Whatever the reason for it - it wasn't true.

Knowing yourself is always a good idea. First of all, we all need to reflect on ourselves from time to time. We all change as life goes on and see what those changes are is good for us to know and understand.

Having a child changes people dramatically. Suddenly, all the irresponsible things we've done aren't things we want to take a chance on anymore. We want to be around for our child. Going to jail, or worse, getting ourselves killed by doing foolish things, isn't worth it anymore.

When looking at yourself, ask questions about who is in your life and why they're there. Ask yourself if they're really fulfilling a need in your life. Are they making your life better? Or is their presence making your life worse? And why?

You might have someone who is hurting you mentally or even physically. How long will you keep dealing with that?

What if this person is one of your own children, then what can you do?

Lots.

Standing up to someone with one or more of the traits of the Dark Triad can be done. Once they know that they can't manipulate you, they change the way they act with you. It doesn't change them completely, but they understand that what they won't work on you.

Take the story of a friend of mine. She had a child whom she caught lying all the time. She'd punished this child over and over for lying. Still, even after growing up and leaving home, he continued to lie.

She came to the conclusion that she'd tried all she knew how to try. She couldn't get him to stop lying, but she could let him know that she was on to him. And she could also let him know that his lies wouldn't work on her.

Sure, she had to get concrete proof of anything he told her. It made things difficult at times too. And when he came home with a woman, he told her he was going to marry. She made sure that the woman knew her son's shortcomings.

Was he angry with his mother?

You bet he was. But she knew it was her responsibility to alert any life partner of his to what he was capable of doing.

She'd figured out that once her son knew people were on to his lies, then he stopped lying to those people. He actually respected the people who called him out on his lies, more than he respected those who fell for them.

With the things in this book, you too can figure out how to call people out on things or simply walk away and leave them to their wrongdoings. It'll all be up to you.

In life, we must pick our battles wisely. We can't fix all the problems in the world. Sometimes it's easier to just walk away from what we can't change, instead of letting that person know we're on to them.

Chapter 1.4. DIY Self-Defense Technique

If you caught your boss in a lie, would you call him on it if it affected others adversely, or would you let it go and why or why not?

Chapter 2

Manipulation and Exploitation - Keep the Distance and Break Free

Knowing when we need to trust our instincts and go with our gut is an essential life skill. Many people play on the emotions of others. It's easy to do to some, and harder to impossible to do to others. That's because some people are more in tune than others. It doesn't make them any smarter, just more wary of individuals and their motives.

If a little girl came crying to you, needing your help to get her poor kitty who is stuck in a tree, you'd probably believe her and rush to help. In this situation, relying on your emotions seems to be the right thing to do.

But if it wasn't a little girl, it was a grown man who came to you, asking for your help to get his stuck kitten, you'd most likely blow him off and assume he had other intentions, perhaps even evil ones.

Not all people react the same way. There are some who might still feel sympathy and empathy for the man – especially if he was very convincing.

Society has taught us to help others. It's a natural human reaction to tend to those who are crying or upset. We want to fix it, most of us want to help. But what happens when someone takes advantage of that part of us? Can we do anything to change the outcome?

You bet we can!

Chapter 2.1. The Home Court Advantage

Beware of the tactic of someone wanting to get you on his turf. Picture this; your boss comes to your office and asks you to come to his office, he'd like to talk to you about something.

Some people would get right up and follow their boss without asking a thing. Others might want to know why the conversation couldn't occur right where they are now.

Savvy people would ask why they need to take the walk down the long hallway when they could talk it right there. That's because they're aware of the home court advantage.

Maybe your boss wants to ask you to do something that's not in your job description. Maybe he wants to ask you questions about a fellow employee he's pretty sure you won't want to give him information on. Whatever his motive is, he isn't wanting to risk having the conversation anywhere but, on his turf, the place he feels the most powerful in.

Before you go to meet anyone in a place you know they feel the most at home in, think about why they want to meet there. You can still go, just be prepared for what they might ask of you and be ready to say no if you feel you should.

Chapter 2.2. Overwhelming Facts and Statistics aka – The Know-it-all

We all know at least one know-it-all. They have an infinite amount of useless knowledge — some of it, even questionable.

Narcissists are the typical culprits who use this sort of thing to make you feel inadequate, undereducated, and sometimes just plain stupid.

You're waiting for a meeting to begin about a promotion that's up for grabs. Your coworker, Mary, is a real piece of work whom you've suspected for some time now to be a narcissist. She smiles at you as you come into the meeting room. "Hi, Lois. You're looking a lot better than the last time I saw you."

You have no idea why that is. "Did I look bad the last time you saw me?"

Her raised brows tell you she's shocked that you didn't already know that. "Oh, I'm sorry. You weren't even aware of it. Forget I said anything. So, I hear this meeting is about the promotion. Mr. Sands is looking for a new admin assistant, is what I heard. He's a real stickler for detail. His sales last year were up eighty percent from the previous five years. That's something, don't you think?"

"I had no idea," is all you can say as you really didn't know a thing about that.

"Of course, you didn't." She smiles, using only one side of her mouth. "Little Lois doesn't ask too many questions. Anyway, Mr. Sands has three kids, sixteen-year-old John Junior, twelve-year-old Tyler, and his wife – June – recently had another child. Finally, a girl. They named her Blanch after his maternal grandmother. She was a nurse in the war."

You're stupefied by all this familiarity she has with the man. "Are you friends with him or his wife?"

"Heavens no." She laughs. "It's common knowledge. But you'd have to ask some questions, and I guess you don't like doing that. It's okay. Not everyone is meant for top jobs. With great pay comes great responsibility. As an admin assistant, I suppose you're aware of how important it is to know all about your boss. You're currently working under, Mrs. Fine. She's a real easy one. My boss, Mr. Crabtree is tough. But he's taught me so much. I couldn't be more thankful. I've got so much experience now; I'm smarter than any Harvard graduate, I can tell you that."

As a matter of fact, Mary can tell you lots and lots of things. Mary can make you feel as if she's so much smarter than you, and that she deserves the job so much more than you do. Mary can make you say that to the person who matters too.

Or you could see what she is doing here, manipulating you to believe she's smarter than you are and deserves to get the better paying job. And you can politely ignore her yammering and do the best you can, using real facts to gain the upper hand and win the job. That's all up to you, and how you decide to roll with the punches, she's throwing your way.

Chapter 2.3. Little to No Time to Make Decisions

Using this tactic, the manipulator has his mind made up. He's just got to get you to agree. But the thing you need to agree on is pretty important, and you don't like the rush he's putting you in.

"Lois, I need you to go ahead and sign the paperwork on the courthouse parking lot. We've got to get it in front of the mayor pronto."

"But that document isn't a thing I've read over yet. I don't want to sign it before I read it."

"It's fine. I've read it. Just sign it, then take it across the street to City Hall."

"If you've read it, then can you at least give me an idea of what it's about? I haven't a clue. I don't want to sign anything that I have no clue about."

"It's about the parking problem at the courthouse. It's not a big deal. Salinas Construction Company has put in a bid to repave it, and it's a fair one. Once you sign the document, we can hire them to repave the parking lot. But you've got to hurry before the mayor leaves for the day."

"I think it can wait. I'd like to read it. And shouldn't we get more bids before we go with anyone?"

"No. Just sign the damn thing!"

The rush makes Lois suspicious. So, she takes the paper, doesn't sign it, but instead does a bit of research. She finds out the coworker is a manipulator who is related to the owner of the construction company and was going to get a kickback for giving them the job. Lois could've been fired for signing the document; thankfully she was smart enough not to let anyone rush her into signing something she hadn't read and researched first.

Chapter 2.4. Using Negative Humor to Disempower

I don't care how much anyone laughs, ugly things someone says about you hurts – and it sticks with you for a very long time.

You will experience this, and you might even dish this kind of humor out at times. It doesn't make it right. As humans, we like to make people laugh. It feels good when everyone around you is cracking up because of something you've said, even when that something might be hurting someone else's feelings.

Being the butt of a joke isn't fun. Even when the butt of the joke is laughing too, they aren't immune to the sting of the negative words.

Young people seem the most prone to doing this sort of thing. As time goes on, and they all find themselves in the prone position as someone roasts them in front of a group, people find it not so funny any longer.

When older adults find it hilarious to make fun of you – especially in front of people – you've got a problem on your hands.

"Sandy, have you gotten the February report yet?"

"Not yet, Mr. Stevens. This computer is giving me fits today."

Sandy's boss narrows his dark eyes at her, his lips pull into a quirky smile. Her skin goes cold as she knows he's about to go off on what he considers a good-hearted roasting of her. What's worse is that there's a lobby full of people waiting to be seen – they'll all hear his harsh but humorous words. Sandy will look like a real jerk if she confronts him for saying the things that make people laugh. If she cries – the way she's wanted to at times when he's done this before – she'll look like a mental case. So, she braces herself and waits.

Mr. Stevens looks at the room full of clients, waiting to be seen. "Allow me to introduce you all to our little secretary, Sandy. You'll have to excuse her this morning. She's got three kids at home that run her ragged. Isn't that right, Sandy?"

She knows where he's going with this and tries in vain to stop it before it can begin, "Oh, they weren't too bad yesterday. It's just the internet. It's slow this morning, is all."

"Yes, well I can see that you at least got to do your hair and makeup today." He chuckles as he looks around the room at everyone, making sure to keep their attention. "Most days, poor Sandy drags in here with her hair in a messy bun atop her head and mascara from the day before puddled beneath her tired eyes. She looks like a raccoon who had a fight with a badger on most mornings."

Everyone laughed, including Sandy who doesn't want to look like a wet blanket. "In my defense, having three kids under the age of five is a lot like living in a den of rattlesnakes. You never know when one is going to go on a biting spree." Sandy wasn't ever the one with the quick wit and snappy responses.

Mr. Stevens loves that about her. "Whatever that means. So, is that big bad internet messing with you today, Sandy?" He scans his audience. "Computers and this one don't get along well. I keep telling her that even monkeys can make computers work. But she refuses to see about getting a monkey to train her."

More laughter, Sandy blushes, feels stupid but laughs along with them. "Yeah, I don't want a monkey to train me."

Hand to the side of his mouth, as if it's a secret, he whispers loudly, "I doubt she'd understand the monkey anyway."

As everyone laughs, Sandy tries to smile, instead of cry. She's taken the man's jabs the whole year she's worked for him. The fear of being fired for telling him off is just too big. She can't risk offending him.

That day she goes home and tells her husband about things for the first time ever. He's angry and wants to confront the man himself. Sandy begs him not to. So, he teaches her how to come back with her own remarks that will sting her boss for a change.

The next morning, Sandy goes into work, feeling confident. Mr. Stevens comes out to the lobby, smiling, ready to give it to her again in front of a brand-new audience. "Morning, Sandy. Has the computer bested you again this morning?"

She's quick to hand him the papers she knew he came for. "Not at all. Why, is yours giving you trouble, sir? I can go take a look at it if you'd like."

"Mine?" He laughs, shakes his head, and seems a little bewildered. "How'd the circus at your home go last night? I bet those kids of yours really stirred things up." He looks at everyone who sits and waits. "Poor Sandy has three kids under five. Her life sounds like a nightmare to me."

"Nightmare?" Sandy says with a laugh. "It's more like a Disney movie, really. When I got home, my hubby had cooked out on the grill while the kids ran around in the yard, burning off some energy. We ate burgers on the deck while sipping on some cold beers. It was nice. Later, the stars came out and my husband and I pointed out the constellations to our budding brood. Then we put the kids to bed and had some alone time, just the two of us, our garden tub, and a bottle of red wine." She shrugs. "But I suppose to you it might seem nightmarish. It's nothing like the bars you spend your evenings after work in. Not that I blame you. Going home to an empty house must feel awful."

Mr. Stevens sails have lost all their wind. "Um, yeah. Well, send in the first client, Sandy."

"Sure thing, Boss." All smiles, Sandy has effectively shut her comedic boss down.

And you can do the same thing too if you'll ignore the jabs you're given and throw a few of your own but in a more positive way.

Chapter 2.5. Consistent Criticism

There are days when you can't seem to do anything right. When you add in a person who constantly criticizes you and everything you do, it makes it so much worse.

"Watch out!" John shouts.

Joe trips over the cables, trying not to fall as he carries the box of receivers. "John, dang, man. Don't shout. You made me trip. I saw the freaking cables, but it was your shouting that screwed me up."

"Sure, it was." John puts the satellite dish on the ground after pulling it out of the truck. "Joe, you're so slow, a sloth seems to be faster compared to you.

If you don't hurry up today, we'll never get the five houses wired for cable."

"We're on time. If you'd shut up and help, we might get done before schedule."

"Hey! What the heck are you doing now, Joe? Put the cable down. It's the wrong one."

"No, it's not."

"It is. You're doing it all wrong."

"Am not." Joe holds up the correct cable. "See, the right one."

"Well, yeah it's the right one now that you put the other one down. I've gotta watch you like a hawk. You get everything wrong."

"Or you could just do your job and leave me to mine." Joe starts to put the cable into the hole John drilled for it.

"Stop!"

Joe's startled. "What?"

"You can't just shove it through there. You've gotta do it easy. Let me show you." He takes the cable out of Joe's hand. "Like this. You were going to do it too fast."

Rolling his eyes, Joe wonders if he'll ever be able to do anything right in the man's eyes.

In situations like these, it's always best to stop the person who's doing this to you right away. Tell them that you will listen to them if they have something constructive to say. Shouting at you will only make it where you don't listen to them at all. And remind them that no one does everything wrong. And no one knows it all either.

Chapter 2.6. The Silent Treatment

I, for one, am a fan of the silent treatment. The quieter it is, the more I like it. If you have someone who does this to you, then I'd like to offer my advice.

Let them shut you out. Let them remain quiet because something you did or said made them angry with you. Relish that silence. It's so much better than their ongoing griping and ridiculing.

When anyone does this to me, and they have – I have a little saying I say to let them know, they ain't getting to me. 'Oh good, the silent treatment. I could use some peace and quiet in my life.'

You've got to remember that they use their silence as a tactic to get to you, to make you feel bad. They want you to miss their presence, miss their acceptance of you. Don't give them what they want. And don't let it get to you. It's not your loss if they keep pulling themselves away and shutting people out.

If you look at what they're doing, they're shutting everyone out, removing themselves from the world. It's really a very self-sabotaging thing to do. When you don't allow yourself to get upset by their actions and really take a look at what they're doing to themselves in a vain attempt to hurt you, you will realize that.

Chapter 2.7. Playing the Victim – Perpetually

This type of mental manipulation is extremely damaging. When the person who has to play the victim is in your life in any capacity, you will find yourself being the villain more than once.

No one likes to be the villain – especially when you really aren't being one.

When confronted with a professional victim, it's important that you let them know you refuse to play the villain in their little mind games. Shut them down quickly and efficiently.

Other ways of playing the victim are to get your sympathy so you'll do something for them. Be wary of this ploy. It happens a lot at work. The victim wants others to do their work and have one sob story after another as to why they need help. Don't fall for it more than once. If they have that much bad luck, there's more wrong with them than what you can fix anyway.

Chapter 2.8. DIY Self-Defense Technique

If you were in a group of people and one of them began to poke fun at someone in your group, would be laughing? Would you join in and poke some fun at the victim too? Or would you stand up to the humorous bully? And why or why not?

Chapter 3

Dark Persuasion – Keep Your Stance

We're bombarded with all sorts of persuasion daily. It's coming at us from all sides. The radio, television, your computer, your cell phone, the people around you, it's all too much!

In this day and age, we have much more persuasive actions coming at us then ever before. That's because there're not only more ways to persuade people, but there are more things to persuade them about.

The in-your-face persuasion isn't so bad. You can take it or leave it, and at least you know what's happening. It's the dark persuasive tactics that you might not even be aware of that matter.

Chapter 3.1. Your Basic Human Rights

First things first, your fundamental rights as a human being. This might seem like a thing that's understood by most people, but that's not always the case. So, we're going to go over what is unequivocally yours.

Knowing what your rights are, gives you that line you can let people know you won't allow being crossed. We have to have lines – all of us do. As children, we learned to test our boundaries. If our parents had little to no boundaries, then we learned little until we became school age. Our peers and teachers would then set the boundaries our parents didn't. Society will always let you know how far you can and can't go. So, letting people know that you know what the socially accepted boundaries are is essential in your role as a citizen of the world.

Another thing that needs to be pointed out about your rights is the fact that you don't have to answer questions anyone asks you about why you feel you have these rights. You have them, end of subject. If someone feels they have to ask you about your rights, they're only trying to get into your head to make you believe you don't actually have the right you're trying to uphold.

Let's talk about your right to life. Not only do you have this right, but you've got the right to live your life in a way that is healthy and happy. If someone is infringing your life that is causing you to be or feel unhealthy or unhappy, you have the unquestionable right to get away from them or make them get away from you – by force if necessary.

What about respect? Do you have the right to be treated with respect by everyone?

You sure do. You should be treated with respect be anyone you first encounter. That is until you do something to lose that respect. The thing is that everyone is given respect in the first place. It's up to you if you can maintain that respect or not. And sometimes, you've got to try to earn it, once it's been lost.

You also have the right to protect yourself from things that threaten to harm you in physical, mental, and emotional ways. This means that if a person is about to punch you in the face, you do not have to stand there and take it.

You've got many possibilities for your recourse. You can hit back. You could dodge the punch. Or you can simply walk away – or run if you feel that threatened. And you can seek help if you feel like you can't face a threat on your own.

Physical violence is easy to see how you've got the right to get away from a person who's threatening to harm you in that way. But what about emotional and mental harm?

The answer to that is, yes. Of course, you have the right to get away from anyone who is threatening or actually harming you in those ways. Again, you can do this on your own, or you might need help. Ask for help if you need it and stay away from the person who tried to or did cause you harm in any of these aspects.

The things you want, the things you have opinions about, and how you feel are also rights that you have. And you've also got the right to have all of these things regardless if anyone else agrees with you or not.

Your opinion might be yours alone. Others might have conflicting opinions. Just as you've got a right to your opinion, they have the right to theirs as well.

You also have the right to make your own priorities. What matters to you the most might not matter to someone else as much or at all. If someone thinks your priorities aren't in line with what they want, that makes no difference. You need to believe in your priorities and stand by them. Don't allow anyone to influence what matters the most to you. A case in point for this is that your boss thinks you should but your job in front of your family. He wants you to change your priorities. You know better than that now, don't you?

It's your right to have your own priorities; no one can make you change them. Again, if you need help getting someone in authority over you to understand and accept this about you, then get the help you need to accomplish that.

If you pay for something, do you feel that you've got the right to have it?

You sure do have that right.

If you pay for gas before going back outside to pump it and there is no gas left to give you, you expect to get your money back, don't you?

And if they refuse to give your money back, you know there are things you can do to get it back. And we're not talking about getting violent here. There are authorities to help you get what you paid for. Use that help if you need it.

And here is a right that many of us don't know that we have. We all have the right to say no. That's not all. We also have the right not to feel even an ounce of guilt for saying, no. Not even an ounce!

That's right. You can say no, and you don't have to say another word after that. You don't have to explain a thing. As a matter of fact, if you want to shut the person bothering you up, simply tell them that it's your right to say no and you're exercising it. Smile, be happy about it. You said, no. And you don't feel bad about doing it either.

Yeah, you!

Chapter 3.2. You Are NOT the Problem

Contrary to what the manipulator wants you to think, *you* are not the problem. You might be their problem as you won't conform to what they want you to, but *you* are not the problem.

A case in point:

"I have asked you time and time again to stop making white rice for dinner. I want mac and cheese."

"For starters, I made both. I don't see why I can't even make what *I* want to eat. You've got what you want. I want what I want."

"Why do you always do this?"

"Do what?"

"Make it all about *you* and what *you* want? What about *me*?"

"What about you? You've got your mac and cheese, don't you?"

"Yeah, but I've gotta smell your disgusting white rice too. It's making me not want to eat my food. You only think about yourself. You're selfish."

"Let me get this straight. *I* made dinner. *I* made what you requested, and now *I'm* the bad guy?"

"Exactly."

"I don't see how you came up with that."

"Because you made me what I wanted, but you sullied it with the smell of that nasty stuff you just had to have. How can you not see it's selfish of you to do such a thing to me?"

Here's what you do in this instance. You take your seat at the table. You eat your white rice without saying a thing. Sure, he's glaring at you – not eating at all. He might even go toss his mac and cheese in the garbage can. He might storm off even.

One thing you know for sure is that *you* are not the problem here.

Chapter 3.3. How to Flip the Script

So, the manipulator in your life has asked you to do something a bit over the top. What can you do to make them see what they're asking is just too much this time?

"Hal, I'm going to need you to take off from work early to come home and mow the backyard."

"I'm not sure if that was a question or not but can't do it. I've got a late meeting."

"I'm sure you can do it. And it wasn't a question. I *need* it mowed."

"And after work just won't cut it for you?"

"I want it done before it gets dark outside. In the morning, I want to sit outside and watch the sunrise."

"The lawn isn't too high to miss the sunrise. You'll be fine, dear. I'll cut it once I get home – even if it's dark out."

"Can't you just do as I've asked you to. Take off early and come home to do it. It's really not a lot I'm asking of you, honey."

"And what is your workday looking like, dear?"

"I've got things to do. And when I get off, I'm going to go get my nails and toes done. So, you see, I can't do it myself. If I could, then I would."

"The nail place isn't open in tomorrow?"

"It is but I wanted to get them done today."

"And I want to attend the mandatory meeting at my job so I can keep my job. So, here's a suggestion. If you want the lawn mowed today, you put your nails off until tomorrow. Otherwise, I'll cut the grass whenever I get home."

"But."

"No, but's, dear. Would *you* take off early and miss a mandatory meeting and risk your job over a freshly cut lawn?"

"Well, no."

"Then why would you expect me to?"

Chapter 3.4. Using Time

As children, time was used to shut us down often. "Mom, can I go to the snake farm with the neighbors? Joe knows one of the guys who works there, and he's gonna let us milk the venom out of the rattlesnakes."

As a mother, the thought of letting your ten-year-old milk a rattlesnake doesn't sit well with you. "Let me think about that for a while, Mike."

"Think about it? That always means no. Aw, come on, Mom – please!"

"I'll have to give it my full attention. I'll let you know what I've decided later."

"But they might leave without me."

"That could happen. I won't hurry to make such an important decision as this one."

"Aw, man."

Chapter 3.5. How to Say No and Mean It

This is a big one. We've all seen the parent getting harassed by their kids. They will say no a thousand times, then finally give in and say yes. Once this has occurred, the kids know that if they can keep up the pressure, they will eventually get their way.

The basic rule here is to never go back on your answer of no. And the secret to this is not to allow anyone to continue to ask the same question you've already given the answer of no to.

The way to enforce this is to add a consequence to asking the same question again. With a child it's easy. 'Ask again, and you won't get any dessert after dinner.'

An adult might be a little harder. If you put your mind to it, I'm sure you can think of something they wouldn't want to give up just so they could bug you about your answer.

Chapter 3.6. Shutting Down A Bully

There are a few lines of thought on this. One of them includes beating the bully up. We don't recommend that one.

Safely shutting down a bully is what we're going for here. In this way, you will utilize the help of others. Go the route of getting others involved, even the authorities if need be. Stand up tall, stay firm.

"Hey, Bozo, you got money. I need five bucks." Josh from the garage comes closer to you as you sit at your desk.

Get up. Place your hands on top of your desk firmly. "Well, I would've been happy to lend you five bucks, but you started off on the wrong foot, Josh. Calling me names won't get you anywhere."

"Sit down and get your wallet out and give me five bucks before I knock your teeth down your throat." He pounds his fist against his palm.

You smile, take out your cell phone and take a quick picture of him doing this. "There we go. You're a physical sign of intimidation has been recorded. And Jane is in the next office. Did you hear Josh threatening me, Jane?"

"Sure did."

"Great." Smiles at Josh. "You might get in a punch, but you'll be spending the night in jail for doing it. Let's not go that route. Like I said, next time, try asking nicely to borrow some money. But don't get mad if I say no. It is my right, after all."

Chapter 3.7. Making the Manipulator Face Consequences

For every manipulative action, there is a consequence. The harshest of them all is the consequence of losing you. You don't use this consequence unless you fully intend to withdraw yourself from the person's life.

The thing about manipulators is that they mentally record every action you do when they've manipulated you or attempted to. If you use the old, I'll leave you, threat and don't stand up to what you've said. They know you never will.

When a manipulator knows you're all talk and no action, you're screwed. You've got to mean what you say, especially with people who manipulate others.

Idle threats will be laughed at, and the manipulation will only get worse. If we're talking about using the manipulative act of bullying, then you've got yourself in a real bind.

If you say you will call the authorities if the bully hits you, and he does go through with the physical harm, you had better call the authorities and let them handle it. Then you better bring down all the consequences on him the law allows.

You might be the one who gets through to him or her that it's just not worth bullying and hurting people physically. You might save their next would-be victim from harm.

If you can come up with consequences for all of the manipulative actions we've gone over, then you can begin to gain control of your life. That's all you're going for anyway. You're not trying to control the manipulator. You're trying to control how you react to those manipulations.

You can't stop the wind from blowing, but you can put on the appropriate attire to help it not affect you so much. You can take your stance against the wind and stay standing. You can't fight the wind any more than you can fight a manipulator.

Just like the wind, a master manipulator will change directions and come at you from another way. They will only do this if they think you've got a weakness, they can take advantage of.

We all have weaknesses; the key to keeping them hidden around manipulators is to watch what you say. Say what you mean, only what you will go through with. Don't let them see you sweat. Don't allow them to think for one moment that they have you on the ropes.

Sure, it might be a ploy at first. The thing is you might only be pretending for the first few times. The times after that, you won't be pretending any longer, you will mean it. And the manipulator in your life will understand that you can't be manipulated.

When you use consequences for the times, they attempt to manipulate you. You not only gain their respect, but you also gain some peace in your life too.

Never fear. If you've been manipulated by someone in your life, there's still hope. You can get a new stand in life. You can show them how you refuse to bend to their manipulations any longer. When you show them that now there are consequences for when they attempt to try to get into your head to make you do what they want, they might try even harder. You'll have to make sure those consequences hurt them where it counts.

Only you really know where it'll sting the most. Only you know what it will take to get them to stop using you as an easy target. Be calm. Be articulate. Be assertive and sure of yourself. You'll be surprised what that can do for you where manipulators are concerned.

Once the manipulator knows you can no longer be his or her victim, they will stop - or they will not have you in their lives anymore. But that's all up to you to make sure they believe you when you say that to them.

Chapter 3.8. DYI Self-Defense Technique

Your spouse wasn't always manipulative but lately, he's started trying to get you to do things he's never done before. He asks you to drop what you're doing to wash his laundry. When you ask what's wrong with him, he tells you that his friend's wife does all his laundry. He wants you to be more like his friend's wife. What do you say to him to make him understand you and he don't have the same type of marriage his friend does?

Chapter 4
Deception – Spot the Attacks

While most people lie at least a few times each day, it's not those little white lies that hurt others. It's the big ones that cause pain and destruction that we need to think about.

Some deceptions occur to keep from hurting someone's feelings. 'Yes, that dress is pretty on you.'

Other deceptions can change your life. 'No, I didn't cheat on you.'

We have lies we tell ourselves too. 'That missing front tooth doesn't look so bad.'

Sometimes we tell lies to help us to try harder at things in life. 'I can achieve the goal of becoming a doctor, even though right now I'm just a receptionist in a doctor's office.'

In this chapter, we want to show you how to spot lies. What the keys are when knowing if a person is being deceitful or not will be revealed. You might think you know all about how liars lie. Let's see if you're right or if you've been deceiving yourself about this.

Chapter 4.1. Omitting Key Details

Leaving out the essential parts of a story is called beating around the bush. You want to bend the truth in such a way that it hides the significant parts of the story.

Martha came home one day and went quietly into the house. Her husband, James asks, "How was your day, honey?"

"Fine." Martha's day wasn't fine though.

"Great. Anything I might be interested in?"

"Nope." She puts her purse away in the top of the hall closet. She doesn't usually do this but doesn't want her husband to find what's inside the purse —

a traffic ticket for rear-ending another car when she failed to stop.

Her husband's phone rings. "It's my cousin, Tony. Hi, what's up, cuz?"

"Is your wife doing okay?" Tony asks.

Martha overhears him and tries to duck out of the room. But James stops her. "Honey, hang on. Tony just asked me if you're doing okay. Why would he ask that?"

She shrugs as Tony says, "Because I saw her on the side of the highway with a cop."

James can't believe it. "Martha, were you on the side of the highway with a police officer?"

"I was." She looks toward the kitchen. "I'm thirsty. Care for a drink?"

"I'm good." James asks Tony, "Did you see anything else?"

"No, just her and the cop is all."

Martha breathes a sigh of relief. The other car must've left by the time Tony saw her. James hangs up, ready to get to the bottom of the story. "Okay, tell me what happened."

"I got pulled over. That's why Tony saw me."

"Why'd you get pulled over?"

She shuffles her feet as she tries to think of a way to not tell him the truth entirely. "Well, I didn't really get pulled over. I was already stopped when the officer came up behind me."

"And why were you stopped."

"I *had* to stop." She fidgets. "Um, it's not a big deal. What would you like for dinner? I'm thinking pasta sounds good."

"Martha! What did you do?" James has just about had it.

"Nothing. It wasn't that bad. Just a little bump. Everyone drove away unharmed." She heads to the kitchen, unable to face her husband any longer.

James gets up and comes to finish their conversation. He takes her by the shoulders, makes her look at him. "Honey, you can tell me anything. Now stop beating around the bush and just tell me what happened."

Knowing she's got to do it sometime, she finally tells him the truth, "I didn't see the car in front of me stopping and hit it in the back bumper. I got a ticket."

"See, that wasn't so hard." James kisses his wife on the forehead. "Are you okay? That's what really matters."

"I'm shaken up. Mostly because I didn't know how to tell you about the incident."

When it comes to telling the truth or lying, lying – or even omitting key details - just prolongs the inevitable.

Chapter 4.2. Giving Too Little Detail

When a person doesn't want to talk about something, especially something you think is important, they can give too little detail to the story to hide the thing they don't want you to know about.

Your husband comes home with a new fishing pole. "That's a nice pole there, honey. How much did that set us back?"

"This thing?" he puts it away in the closet quickly. "Not much. Is dinner ready?"

"Not yet. Just waiting on the biscuits to cook. So, how much was it?"

"Boy, am I tired. I went to buy the pole and spent way too much time in line at the store."

"And how much money did you spend on the pole?"

"Oh, I saw my old friend, Grady there too. He said to tell you hi. He and his wife might join us at the Easter celebration downtown next month. Do you think those biscuits are done yet? I'm starving."

"Sure, just tell me how much that fishing pole was."

"I think I left the receipt in the car. I'll have to get it later – after dinner."

"Give me a ballpark figure then."

"Um, less than what I paid for your last hair and nail appointment."

"That was quite a bit."

"Yes, it was."

"So, are you going to tell me how much you spent of our money or not?"

"Probably not. Let's eat."

Chapter 4.3. Giving Too Much Detail

When someone is going to lie, premeditating the lie, they might make up a lavish story. This story will have endless details that are meant to make the story sound believable, but it only serves to make the listener sure the story is made up.

The liar has rehearsed this story over and over again in their minds. In their opinion, it's the details that make it so believable.

John was supposed to be out looking for a job. He's living with his brother, Jay and it's been going on six months now that he's been unemployed.

Coming through the door, looking worn out, John falls onto the sofa. "What a day."

"I hope you had at least one interview today, John," Jay says.

"One?" He shakes his head. "Try three. And boy what a day this was. First of all, I got up late. My alarm didn't go off. And to top that off, my socks were still wet. I could swear I turned the dryer on last night. I guess I didn't though. The socks were still too wet to wear, so I had to wait thirty minutes to let them dry."

"You could've borrowed a pair of mine."

"Nah, that's asking too much." Joe puts his feet up on the coffee table. "So, I went to get into my car and guess what?"

"What?"

"The cat was inside of it again. He peed all in it too. That really made me mad, so I was in a bad mood already. But I went out searching for a job anyway."

"Good. And how did that go?"

"Breakfast was a flop. Jason at the burrito barn gave me bacon instead of sausage. I had to eat it anyway as I'd already driven off. And I noticed the sign had been changed to blue. Did you notice that?"

"No, I did not."

"Yeah, it's blue now. You can go check if you want to. It's blue."

"I don't really care about that. Did you get a lead on a job or not?"

"I'm getting to that. So, the first stop was at Carlton's spa."

"Why would you apply at a spa, Joe? You're not exactly spa material. Your last job was working at the dairy, milking cows."

"They have excellent benefits is why I applied there, Jay. I researched that spa and found out it's in the top one hundred places to work in this town. The average employee makes twice as much as people do at any other spa in this area. So, it made perfect sense to apply there."

"So, did you get the job?"

"I wish. I forgot my driver's license at home. They couldn't even do an interview without me having that. They said next Tuesday at three I can come in. I've got to bring my resume too."

"I've never been asked for my driver's license before doing an interview in my entire life. And why wait until a week from now anyway?"

"They've got renovations to deal with. And plus, there's a girl going out on maternity leave that makes the appointments for interviews. So, that's why."

"You said you applied at two other places, right?"

"Yeah, those places had the same problem. No one will interview me without me having that dang license. I can't believe I forgot it today. Wasted so much dang time."

Jay sighed, feeling like the last thirty minutes of his life, listening to all the bologna his brother had spewed had wasted his time too. It was obvious to him that his brother hadn't done a thing he'd said he had. Well, except getting that burrito.

Chapter 4.4. Recalling Every Last Detail

Saying way too much shows the listener that the speaker has rehearsed this story many times. Again, the use of details most people wouldn't bother with shows us the lair believes throwing them in makes them sound believable.

"I was only going thirty-three miles an hour, officer."

"How are you sure of that exact number?"

"I always go that exact speed whenever I am driving on a suburban street is why. See, I go fifty-seven on the highway. And when it's raining, I go forty-two."

"So why did my speed gun show me that you were going forty?"

"It must be broken. I've heard about that before. It was in the Daily Bugle last week. You can't count on speed guns to be accurate. The Durant 44 is especially faulty. Is that the brand you have?"

"Um, yeah, it is."

"Yes, I thought as much. I've seen this before. You shouldn't bother giving me a ticket. A judge will just throw it out."

"You sound like this has happened to you before."

"A few times."

"Yeah, I bet it has."

This person had their story down pat so they could speed and get away with it.

Chapter 4.5. Avoiding Face to Face Conversations

Most people avoid uncomfortable situations if they can. When someone knows they've done something wrong and don't want to face the consequences, they might try to avoid meeting face to face with whomever they've wronged.

Lying is easier done by some people when done over the phone.

Mr. Davenport has found a discrepancy in the financial paperwork and is wanting to meet with the employee who filled out the document. "Harvey, we need to meet this afternoon."

"Sure, why?" Harvey asks over the phone.

"The financial report is off. How about we meet after lunch?"

"No can do, boss. I've got an appointment with the dentist. How about we just talk about it over the phone?"

"I'd like to meet in person."

"I'm afraid that won't be possible."

"We can do it tomorrow if you've got an appointment today."

"Oh, tomorrow is no good either. I've got to be in Washington. My brother is graduating from college."

"In March? Where's he graduating from?"

"A small, private college."

"Okay, Monday then. Bright and early."

"How about we just talk now? We can deal with this over the phone. No reason to meet in person. I can tell you whatever you want to know over the phone."

It seems Harvey doesn't want to face his boss. He must've done some real bad stuff on the financial report.

Chapter 4.6. The Long Pauses

This type of tactic is more common than most. The deceiver isn't good at lying. It takes him or her time to come up with something that sounds like it could be the truth.

"So, did you see my favorite coffee mug, Damian?"

"Hm," he hums as he taps his chin. "Let me think about that for a minute. Did I see your favorite coffee mug? You mean the one with Dad's face on it, don't you?"

"Yes, the one I use every, single day. It was on the shelf, and now it's not. And you were the only one home. So, have you seen it?"

"Well, I'm not sure." He pauses - and waits and waits while tapping his chin.

"Damian, it's a simple yes or no answer I'm looking for. Did you see it or not?"

"I'm trying to remember, Mom. Can't you give me a second to think about it?"

She could give him a year. He's going to say he didn't see it. That's because he broke it and has already gotten rid of the evidence, he's just trying to buy himself some time to come up with a great story that clears him from all wrong-doing.

Chapter 4.7. Making Sure the Blame Isn't on Them

When people refuse to take responsibility for what they've done wrong, they will grasp at everything they can to prove they're not to blame.

"Who broke my favorite coffee mug?"

Damien looks at the broken pieces of the mug he was sure he'd gotten rid of. "Where did you find those?"

"Out by the dumpster." She shakes them at him. "Who broke this?"

"Not me. I didn't do it."

"Then who did?"

"I was in the shower all morning. It couldn't have been me."

"You were the only one home, Damian!"

"I know. But I was in the shower, Mom. I have no idea what happened to your favorite coffee mug. It wasn't me."

Sure, it wasn't.

Chapter 4.8. Shifting from Past to Present Tense

You've got to really listen hard to spot a liar doing this. Moving from past tense to the present means the person is getting into their brain – reliving the story they've made up to cover up what they've done.

Jane says she was the victim of a robbery when she was going to deposit the money from the bakery she worked as a manager for.

The officer questions her about what happened, "So, you got to the ATM machine and put the bank card in then punched in the pin, right?"

"Yes, I did that. I put the money bag on the passenger seat. The deposit slip was already made out. I'd done that at the bakery before I'd left. It was crazy. I was sitting there, then he jumps out of nowhere. He holds his gun right in my face. I scream, and he tells me to shut up."

She tells the story as if she sees it. Because in her mind, she sees this story she's made up.

It takes a keen ear to pick up on the change in tense and why a person would do such a thing. When people are telling the truth, especially about a situation like a robbery, they tend to stick with the most important details and speak in the past tense, since it already happened.

Chapter 4.9. Answering a Question with One of Their Own

The tactic of answering a question with a question buys the lair time to come up with something plausible. They're not the type to let the silence go by, so they fill it with something that can't be used against them.

"Damien, did you break my coffee mug?"

"Did *I* break your coffee mug?"

"Yes. You were the only one home."

"*Was I* the only one home? Like, how do you *know* that for sure?"

"Because only your father, me, and you live here is why. So, did you break it or not?"

"*Me*? Why could it only have been *me*? What if someone else came in here while I was in the shower?"

"Why would anyone come into our home, come to this shelf and take my favorite mug off and drop it on the floor?"

"Is that what happened? Was it dropped on the floor?"

"I assume so."

"But didn't you find the broken pieces outside by the dumpster?"

"Yes. Obviously, someone had cleaned the pieces up and put them out there. Who could've done that?"

"How should *I* know?"

It's enough to make you want to pull your hair out!

Chapter 4.10. Beware the Oaths

The old, I swear on a stack of Bibles tactic. What people will say to try to get themselves off the hook is insane.

"Damian, I know you broke my coffee mug. Now just admit it so we can move on from this insanity. Please!"

"Mom, cross my heart and hope to die. I didn't break it."

"You had to have been the one to do it. No one else was here."

"If you want to get me a stack of Bibles, I'll put my hand down on top of them and swear on them all. Mom, I didn't do it. You can trust me. I'm not a liar. I'm better than that. I swear that to you."

He can swear all day; it won't make anyone believe he didn't break the cup.

Chapter 4.11. DIY Self-Defense Technique

How important is it to you that you get to the bottom of things and make someone tell you the truth when you are sure they're lying?

Chapter 5

Covert Hypnosis - Keep Your Balance

While a person must be aware of the usual type of hypnosis, covert hypnosis is a thing done to you, and you're unaware of what's happening. You may never know if you've been covertly hypnotized or not. Chances are though that you've experienced things then later wondered why in the world you participated in that thing or acted the way you did.

Those who seek to used covert hypnosis on you to get you to do what they want, generally won't want to let you in on what they did to you. It's not like they have to use a pocket watch to put you under their spell, they use words, emotions, and actions to get you under their spell.

Often times, the reasons to hypnotize you are to get you to do darker things than you normally would. Other times, it may be used to distract you from something so they can get away with what they've done. Whatever the reason is, you can bet it's never a good one. If it was, then the hypnotist would be happy to let you in on what they're doing to you.

Chapter 5.1. Beware Complete Absorption

Have you ever felt as if you were being pulled into someone's story?

Maybe you've met someone at some point in your life who could tell you things so vividly it made you see what they were saying in your mind. Their words might've ignited emotions within you. Maybe you could even smell the things they were talking about – the fresh bread they spoke of baking.

If you can recall a time like this, then you can safely say that you've been hypnotized covertly. You have been pulled into a place the speaker wanted you, without you even knowing you were about to embark on a journey at all.

You hadn't expected to be seeing things so vividly, you hadn't opened a book or turned on the television, yet there you were, seeing it all unfold in front of you. It felt as if you'd experienced it with the person, even though you'd never left where you stood.

When you find yourself taking the word of what the speaker is saying, you aren't using your own mind – your analytical mind. When you allow this to happen to you, your brain takes in what's being said as truth. This is dangerous.

Sally went with her friend Bonnie to a huge, non-denominational church service one night. She was feeling skeptic about the service as Bonnie claimed she actually felt what the speaker talked about. He was so well-spoken and charismatic that his words left you feeling wonderful.

Sally wanted to see for herself if she would be taken by the charm of this speaker.

The crowd alone told Sally that many people believed the same way her friend did. "You all are a bunch of sheep. Can't you tell by the atmosphere that this man is setting you up so he can fill your mind with whatever he wants to?"

"He's not a bad man, Sally. Give him a chance." Bonnie was all smiles, ready and willing to accept whatever the man said, and Sally could see that.

"Why don't you try to listen to what he says without letting your emotions get involved?" Sally recommended. "Take notes of what he's saying then go home and research his claims. Don't just take his word for it."

"Research?" Bonnie shook her head. "Nah, that takes too much time. He's already done all that. That's why he's telling us, so we don't have to waste our time."

Sally crossed her arms in front of her, taking the position to guard herself against being taken in by the man. As the lights began to fade, the music came to a crescendo; then a spotlight shone on the man her friend had told her about.

Good looks, a nice suit, and a smile that most likely had cost him a pretty penny, the man was more than easy on the eyes. But Sally wasn't one to be taken in by a pretty face. "Sure, he's good-looking, but that doesn't mean he can be trusted."

"He's smart and inciteful too though," Bonnie argued.

"We'll see." Sally wasn't about to fall for the man's words.

"Good evening, everyone. Thank you for coming out to see me tonight. I've got so many wonderful things to share with all of you. Theres many new and useful things you need to hear."

Sally frowned as she shook her head and looked around at all the people who already hung on every word he said. "This man could say the Earth is flat and everyone in this giant stadium would believe him, accept me."

The man had a story for each new thing he wanted his flock to know. Vivid details took the audience on a journey; only Sally alone seemed not to be going on.

She heard words that pulled at her mind to follow but refused to allow it to go. Sally wondered why the man was so against some companies, telling stories about how they'd ruined people's lives and were killing the planet.

One of the companies was her favorite candy company. She knew Bonnie even had a bar of chocolate in her purse from the company. The only thing he'd said about it was that they had used cocoa from a country that used little children to harvest it.

As they were leaving that night, Sally saw many people throwing away the candy they had that the company had made, including Bonnie. "Yuck! It's disgusting what the makers of this candy are doing. I'll never buy another thing from them."

"We aren't sure what he said was true, Bonnie. Don't be so quick to judge when you don't have the facts," Sally cautioned her friend.

That night, Sally got right on her computer and began looking up all the things the man had said. While some things were true, they'd been exaggerated. And other things had no basis of truth at all.

Bonnie still argued, "Why would he lie, Sally? What good would it do him?"

"He's just happy to get lots of people to do anything he says, is why. And once he's got enough of you sheep following him, he can do things that others can't. He can use his hold over you all to his advantage; he can threaten large entities if he wants to. I'm sure there's a financial aspect too. Just listen to your mind, Bonnie. He's playing on your heart and emotions. Don't let him. By the way, how much money did you drop in the collection plate tonight?"

"He says we should put in ten percent of what we make. I put a hundred in the plate since I make a thousand a week."

"So, he gets a lot of you guy's money, and he has you all in the palm of his hand too. See how attractive that is?" Sally could only shake her head as she knew it would take something very upsetting to get her friend not to buy into the man anymore. She'd been covertly hypnotized, and it wouldn't be easy to get her to come out of it as long as she still went to listen to the man.

Chapter 5.2. A Vivid Imagination Can Get You into Hot Water

If you're one of those people with what some call an overactive imagination, you better watch out for those people who will see it and exploit it. It's relatively easy to get people with vivid imaginations to fall for things. After all, they can picture what the speaker is saying. Their emotions get all caught up in stuff without them even meaning to.

Myra had an agenda when she came into work as a small grocery store clerk. She and her boyfriend had planned on robbing the store, but they didn't want to attract attention the way some robbers would.

She had the job of getting her boss out of the store. She was banking on his vivid imagination to get this to happen, so her boyfriend could come in and take the things they'd planned on taking.

The couple only needed a few minutes to get things done. This meant the owner didn't need to be gone long at all.

Coming in, looking worried, Myra didn't greet the owner as she usually did. "Mr. Baker, doesn't your daughter drive a red Chevy minivan?"

"Yes."

"Oh no! I thought she did. I saw a terrible accident on my way in. It's right off the highway. I hope it's not her." Myra held in the smile that tried to creep onto her lips as she saw the horror in her boss' eyes. She knew right where his daughter was. In her History class in the high school, she'd passed on her way to work.

"She should be in school though," he said, but the look in his eyes told Myra he wasn't so sure of that.

Myra knew the man's daughter had been skipping school lately and getting into trouble with a crowd her family didn't care for. "Maybe you should go see if it's her or not, sir."

Moving quickly, he headed to the door. "I'll be back as soon as I can."

With him gone, the couple now could take whatever they wanted. She'd accomplished her mission by using the man's vivid imagination against him.

Chapter 5.3. No Questions Asked

What would happen if we all just believed what anyone said?

In the past, it was taken for granted that whatever was written in school books was true. And whatever you read in a newspaper or saw on the news was also true. With the vast amount of information available to all of us now, we've found that not to be true.

So, if we have to second guess the news media now, shouldn't we do the same for any other information we're given?

Sandra had an expensive purchase to make. She needed a new car. While she didn't have enough money to get a brand new one, she could afford a nice used one. But counting on the salesman, to be honest with her was a thing she didn't have much confidence in. "I know you say it doesn't have any mechanical problems, but it's ten-years-old, there's got to be some issues this car has gone through. I wanted to get something newer and with a lot fewer miles on it too."

"But this one will work perfectly for you." It was pretty evident that the salesman wanted to get the older car off his lot, and he'd love it if he were able to sell it for more than it was worth too.

Sandra could do the not so intelligent thing and not ask the man any questions about the car. She could just take his word for it. If she did that, she might drive off in a real clunker though.

Chapter 5.4. Don't Get Emotionally Involved

It's hard to be a caring person without getting duped a time or two. Getting emotionally involved with the wrong people can hurt you in more ways than one.

Take Sylvia, for example. Sylvia was a new property manager for an apartment building. It was her first job as a manager, and she was excited about the whole aspect of it.

When rent time came around, most of the renters came in and paid on time. But one of them came in with a sob story. "It's nice to meet you, Miss Sylvia. I'm Collette. I wish I could be meeting you on better terms; unfortunately, this isn't so. My cousin came down with the mumps last week. I had to miss work to go tend to her five children."

"How awful," Sylvia says as she too had the mumps last year and knew how horrible it can be. "Since you missed work, are you having trouble coming up with the rent money?"

"I sure am. I don't suppose you can give me a week to get it."

"I'm new here. I'm not sure if my boss will allow that. Is there anyone you can borrow the money from?"

Shaking her head sadly, she answers, "No, ma'am. I'm in a rough patch here. My family moved out of town last year. I'm alone here now."

"Well, that cousin you helped out might be able to help you," Sylvia offers.

"No, she's broker than I am – and I am broke." She smiles, reassuringly. "If you give me a week, I promise you I'll have it. Miss Sandy used to work with me all the time. She can vouch for me."

Sylvia knows the prior manager was fired. She wasn't sure why that was but giving tenants too long to pay their rent might've been it. "I wish I could help you. It's just that I'm new. I don't know what I can do for you."

Not expecting the woman to get out of the chair and fall on her knees, Sylvia is at a loss as Collette pleads, "Please, Miss Sylvia. I'm desperate here. I'll do anything you ask me to. Clean your office. Mow the grass. Anything. Just please give me a week."

Getting up to help the poor woman up, she decides to help her out. "Okay, look, I'll pay the difference for you and you can pay me back. How much are you short?"

"All of it."

"You don't have a dime to your name is what you're saying?"

"Not a dime."

Feeling horrible for the woman, she helps her sit back down then goes to take her seat. "I'll see how long I can hold my boss off. Do your best to get the money by next week."

"Thank you!"

Later that night, Sylvia and her husband go out to dinner at a local bar and grill. The sound of a woman laughing catches her attention. When she follows the voice, she finds Collette playing a game of pool – a beer in her hand and a smile on her lips as she tells her friends, "The next round is on me.

I've got my new landlady wrapped around my little finger."

Chapter 5.5. Don't Forget to Evaluate Your Decisions

When making important decisions, it's crucial to take a moment or even longer to really think about things before you make the final decision. You can't just go on anyone's word after all. You've got to take the time to research and find things out on your own.

Jana was about to buy a home in a town she'd never lived in before. She was doing everything online and using a realtor she'd never even met in person. The house seemed almost too good to be true. A large Victorian home was a thing she'd found online, and it was selling for cheap.

Jana had plans of opening bed and breakfast in the home. It would be her home and her business. But she wasn't taking the time to check things out and evaluate her final decision. Excitement filled her with the promise of owning her first home and business, all in one.

When her sister called to see how things were going, she answered the call excitedly, "Hi. Guess what I'm doing."

"I've got no idea. What are you doing," her sister asked?

"I'm buying a Victorian mansion. I'm going to make it into bed and breakfast too."

"Wow. I'd love to see it. Where's it at?"

"Houston."

"Texas?"

"Yes."

"You live in Ohio. When did you go see it?"

"I haven't yet."

"But you'll go see it before you buy it, right?"

"No. The entire deal is going to be done online. I'm about to make the down payment today. Then the realtor will send me all the papers to sign, and I'll be a homeowner and soon to be a business owner too!"

"Did you have anyone check this house out for you?"

"The realtor handled all that."

"You need to take a moment and really think about this, sis. You're trusting this one person to do right by you. It's a bit much; don't you think?"

"Why would he lie to me about the condition of the property?"

"Why *wouldn't* he, is the better question. Let me help you find out more about this before you go and sign any papers or spend any money, okay?"

"I really want to do it now. I trust the man."

"Please, take a moment to think, sis. The house isn't going anywhere, right?"

"He said there were other interested buyers. That's why there's a rush."

"Sounds like a scam to me. Come on, let me help you check things out. You don't want to get yourself into a terrible situation, do you?"

After a week of fact-checking and making a visit, Jana was happy she followed her sister's advice. The pictures the man had sent her weren't anywhere near what the house really looked like. And she couldn't find the company he said he worked for either. She'd taken just enough time to evaluate her final decision, and she made a great one by not going through with the bad deal.

Chapter 5.6. DYI Self-Defense Technique

You pull up at a gas pump to get gas when a woman approaches you, asking for money to buy her baby some milk. Do you blindly give her money, or do you check out her story first? Or do you go inside the store and buy the milk then give it to her? Do you just say no? And why did you make the decision you made?

Chapter 6

Brainwashing – Keep Your Stance

Although it's unlikely that you will ever face being brainwashed, it's nice to know what to look for if someone is attempting to put you under their control.

Most brainwashers start out slowly, using systematic approaches to gain your trust and also begin the process of breaking you down. It sounds crazy to think that anyone would hang around a person who was doing things to break them down.

Not every person will hang around for another person to wear them down then build them back up again in the image they want. But some people have little to no friends or family. Some people are desperately alone and seek friends wherever they can.

Being desperate for attention makes you an easy target for any manipulator. Another thing that makes a person an easy target is being a naiveté. You may have lots of friends, but you might be naïve, and that alone makes you an easy target for those seeking to use you.

And why does anyone want to use another person in the first place?

You guessed it. Monetary gains. This can be money, but it can also be work. Some even do it just for the thrill of being able to bend someone so wholly to their will.

How they do, it is pretty straightforward and simple. They spot the victim. The person has to be ripe for the picking. Once they have that person in their sights, they swoop in. Either charming and charismatic or quiet and looming near the intended victim, they stalk their prey.

Once they get to talking to you, they will build you up; flattery is used to make you think that they think a lot of you. But after a while, and by a while I mean weeks, months, or even years, they will begin the process of tearing you down.

"Your hair is looking thin and greasy. What have you been doing to it? You should let me help you find some things to make it look better."

"You're gaining a lot of weight. You should let me help you diet."

"You're mismanaging your money. I guess you just don't have the mental capacity to handle it. You should let me deal with your finances."

The first thing you allow them to help you with gives them the in they need. First, it's your haircare. Next, it's what you eat and how often you exercise and what kinds of exercises you do. Then it's handing every paycheck over to them to let them handle your money. It just keeps going on and on until you are handing them everything and every last power you have – and you are doing it on what seems like your own free will.

In this chapter, you will read some cases where people became the victims of brainwashers.

Chapter 6.1. You are Not Who You Think You Are

Not so much when we're young and growing, but once we've matured, we have a pretty good idea of who we are and what we stand for. Again, not everyone will stay around someone who says bad things to them – but some will.

The brainwasher will say all sorts of things to make their victim believe they're not as smart as they thought they were. They'll make them think twice about everything that comes out of their mouth. They'll have good reason to do those things as the brainwasher constantly corrects them, even when they thought they were right.

Joy had just gotten out of a bad marriage. Her husband hadn't ever mistreated her, but he did cheat on her. It left her feeling bad about herself.

She couldn't figure out what she'd done to make the man she loved, go out and find random women to cheat on her with.

Joy also had no idea how much her insecurities showed. When Randy, a charming older man, introduced himself to her at the local grocery store in the produce department, she had no idea he'd seen weakness in her. She was ripe, ready for the picking for what he had in mind.

Randy wasn't looking for money. Randy was looking for a woman to do all he needed to be done – and he didn't like to ask anyone to do anything more than one time.

He asked her out to dinner, told her she was just about the most beautiful woman he'd ever laid eyes on.

Joy was flattered and decided to go out with the man – even though she wasn't completely herself yet.

Being in a marriage for five years had Joy missing the comfort of having someone around when she got home each evening after work. And the bed was the worst place in her home. It felt so empty and only reminded her that her husband had found other women he wanted to take to his bed.

She'd been sleeping on the sofa until Randy came into her life. He too had been in a marriage which had ended when his wife died in an accident a few years earlier. He also missed having someone around. He too didn't like sleeping alone.

Out of loneliness, Joy moved way too fast with the man she barely knew. He'd lived in another town, and no one in her town knew of him. He'd moved into town with his job as a fireman. His rugged good looks and great physique didn't hurt things at all. Joy was enamored with him rather quickly.

After moving in together after only a week, Randy told Joy he didn't really think she should have to work. He made plenty of money, and she should quit her job and just relax.

Joy didn't know what to do. She liked her job and her coworkers. Plus, she liked the independence having her own money gave her. But Randy struck a nerve when he told her that her husband had probably strayed because she worked and couldn't give him as much attention as he'd needed.

Randy explained that he just didn't want anything to get in the way of their budding relationship. He thought that he might be falling in love with her.

Hearing this and coupling it with how she might've been somewhat at fault for the destruction of her former marriage, Joy agreed to quit her job and stay home.

She vowed to her coworkers who were also her friends that they'd still keep in touch and hang out together often. Joy found it kind of fun staying home all day. Doing the chores like the laundry, folding and putting away Randy's clothes, was oddly comforting. She had a man in her life again – a good man – a man who thought about her all the time and wanted her with him as much as possible. It was sweet.

When Joy and some friends from her old job went out for lunch, she came home to find Randy had come home early. He was not happy that she wasn't there when he got home.

Even though she'd done nothing wrong, Joy felt guilty for not being there for Randy. She apologized and told him the next time she was going to go out with her friends; she'd ask him what time he'd be getting off, so she'd be there for sure.

Even though Randy agreed that it was a great idea, he wasn't happy with her having friends, but didn't tell her that. He knew how he'd get in between her and her friends anyway.

A week later, Joy called Randy to ask when he'd be home. Her friends called and would love it if she could meet them for lunch. Suddenly, Randy had things he needed her to do for him, and then he'd come home early. "Sorry, today's just not good, honey."

And this kept on happening until Joy's old friends stopped inviting her out at all. Now she was home – alone all day. She ate more than usual, and Randy confronted her about her weight gain. He made a diet and exercise regimen she had to follow. He kept finding things wrong with Joy that he corrected all the time.

Joy felt like a hamster on a wheel. She was going and going – but didn't ever get anywhere. Her mind wasn't nearly as sharp as she'd remembered it being. She'd been active, smart, happy; she knew she had.

Randy's answer when she asked him if he thought something was wrong with her, "I think you must've seen yourself in a different light than what the reality is. Honey, you're just not that smart. Your kind of lazy too. And to be honest, you have pretty low self-esteem. It's okay with me; I love you just the way you are. You're a great little homemaker. As a matter of fact, I think it's time I put a ring on your finger and marry you. We can start having kids right away. Won't that be great?"

Joy wasn't sure that would be great at all. "I think I might need some time alone, Randy. I think I'm kind of falling apart. You don't want to marry me like this."

But he did want that. He was waiting to break her down entirely before marrying her and having kids with her. Now, he could control her; he could control what happened with their children. He was in control of it all, and he'd put time into her. He wasn't about to let her go now - unfortunately for Joy.

Chapter 6.2. Using Guilt to Break You Down

Lisa and Frank had been married for a few years when he began to change. He'd been working as a correctional officer for ten years, and suddenly he was just done with it. "I don't want to be there anymore, Lisa."

"My income isn't enough to support our family, Frank. You can quit once you have another job to go to. It's the responsible thing to do. We've got kids to think about, Frank."

"So, what you're saying is that it doesn't matter to you if I have to go every day to a job I hate?" he asked, hurt filling his eyes.

Immediately guilt filled her. "No. I just mean that you need to find another job before you quit this one. You're the one with the health insurance. I only work part-time, and they won't give me any more hours."

"Why don't *you* find another job then, Lisa?"

She liked her part-time job. "Frank, my job allows me to be there for the kids whenever I need to. When they're sick, I can stay home and take care of them. And I'm off early enough to pick them up from school too. I like my job."

"Well, I hate mine. I think you're really selfish, Lisa. It's all about you and what you want and to hell with me." He storms off, leaving Lisa unsure of what to do – the guilt is almost overwhelming.

A month later, Frank calls her to let her know he had an accident at work. He's in the hospital, he fell and hurt his back. He's not sure he can even go back to work now.

It's all on Lisa's shoulders now. She feels terrible that it's come to this. And she feels like his accident is her fault in a way. He'd said he hated his job. Maybe he wasn't as careful as he should've been. Perhaps he was so desperate to get out of the job that he'd do anything – even intentionally hurt himself.

Even thinking that way about her husband bothers her. So, Lisa gets a full-time job with benefits, and Frank stays home. He spends most of his time on the couch, watching television. He's not in any kind of shape to do anything for the kids. And when Lisa looks the least bit put out when she has to do everything, he tells her how selfish she is and how he's hurt and can't do anything right now.

Day after day, nothing changes. Frank never seems to get any better. He refuses to go see the doctor again, calling them all quacks who don't know a thing. He's sorry, but Lisa will just have to keep on doing what she's doing.

It's wearing her down; she's exhausted all the time. But if she says the slightest thing about it, Frank says something to make her feel guilty. She just keeps going, doing everything while he does nothing, and she can't stop feeling guilty for all of it.

Chapter 6.3. Betraying One's Self

When the brainwasher is also your kidnapper, you might find that you will betray yourself and fall for the kidnapper. It might seem impossible, but it has happened before.

"Greg, let me out, please. It's been weeks that you've kept me in this cage." Gina is about to go insane if she can't be set free.

Greg can see how fragile she is now. It's time to give her his sob story. "Look, I'm not an evil man. I wasn't always this way. My mother – well, she did horrible things to me when I was just a kid. It made it hard for me to learn in school. I had no choice but to turn to a life of crime to make money. But I never meant to hurt you. I only had to take you to make your father pay for your release. It seems he cares about as much for you as my mother cared for me."

"He still hasn't sent anything?" she asks.

"Nothing."

"Your mom was really bad to you?"

"Horrible."

"Wanna tell me about it?"

As Greg lets her into his very troubled mind, Gina finds empathy with the man, then love for him. And it's all downhill from there.

Chapter 6.4. A Crisis of Identity

Sometimes when the victim falls in love with the brainwasher, they can find themselves unsure of who they are anymore. They no longer feel like their old selves. In their mind, they're new and improved. They want to find the new person they've become, and sometimes they even change their names to take on an entirely new identity.

Chapter 6.5. Let Me Help You

Everyone needs help now and then. It's okay to accept help when you really need it. But when someone constantly jumps in to help you, they're not really trying to help you. They're trying to make you dependent on them.

Think about two-year-old's and how they will kick up a fuss when you're trying to help them do something. It's in our biological makeup to want to do things for ourselves. We need some independence.

You have to remember that when someone is doing everything for you, what are you doing? I'll tell you what you're doing; you're sitting there, wondering why you did it wrong, and someone else has to do it for you. You sit there and wonder what is wrong with you – and that's precisely what the brainwasher wants. They want you to think you're inadequate and that you need them.

Chapter 6.6. Accepting Their Ideas

Stan is putting the dishes away that his wife asked him to. But then she comes in and puts her hand on her hip, asking, "Why are you putting them in that cabinet?"

"This is where we've always put them."

"I want them under the cabinet now. It makes more sense that way. Move them."

"I don't think it makes more sense at all. I'm leaving them right where they've always been."

"Move them." She points at the bottom cabinet. "Think about it for a minute. You never stop and think. You always think you know it all. The grandkids are coming. If the dishes are up there, they won't be able to reach them. So, putting them low enough for them to get them makes perfect sense. See?"

"Yeah, now I do."

It still makes no sense, but she talked circles around him until she had him agreeing with her.

Chapter 6.7. Choosing to Live A Good Life – Or the Brainwasher's Idea of One Anyway

Nancy lived in a nice home with her family, but lately, she's been hanging out a lot with her friend from her school days who lives in a commune with a lot of other people. "It's so peaceful out here, Nancy. And we all get along so well. You should really come to join us."

"Yeah, but you all have to put your money together. And you all have to make your money by baking bread and then going to town to sell it door to door. It's not my kind of thing."

"Baking bread and helping people get something that's actually good for them – way more nutritious than what they can get from the grocery store – isn't your thing?"

"Well, when you put it like that, I guess it's not as lame as I thought."

"And living here, all together, sharing everything is pretty awesome. I mean, your house is okay and all but here we sit and look at the stars while our leader, Joe, tells us stories. Then we all go to our beds and sleep peacefully all night long. It's a much better way of life. I'm never sorry I left home."

"It does sound nice."

Being controlled is never nice for long.

Chapter 6.8. DYI Self-Defense Technique

If someone were to tell you ugly things about yourself would you head their words and try to make changes to yourself or would you blow them off and boot them out of your life? Why or why not?

Chapter 7

Mind Games – Dominate the Battle Ground

It's not always easy to see when someone is playing mind games with you. If they're adept at it, it's nearly impossible to see it, until it's too late. In this chapter, we'll look at different ways people can play with your head. Maybe it'll help you figure it out a lot sooner when someone's playing with your mind.

Chapter 7.1. Guilt

When someone knows they've got to ask you something you will not want to do, they start thinking of a way they can get you to do it anyway.

Lila has three kids, and she needs a babysitter for the entire weekend. The man she's had her eye on for months, Jeff, has finally asked her out and it's for a weekend getaway. She can't miss this golden opportunity.

But Lila's kids are bad. Really bad. She's never disciplined them in their short lives. All of them are small and cranky and mean. Her sister has watched them for short spurts of time but not even overnight before as they're just too bad.

But Lila is desperate as she goes to see her sister with the kids in tow. "Hey, Lola. How are you doing today?"

"Fine." Lola eyes the kids. "You taking the kids for a walk or something?"

"I'm trying to tire them out. I've been doing everything I can to get them to sleep the whole night. It's been working so far. A nice long walk after dinner and they take baths then go right to bed. I think I've finally got this mother thing licked."

"Good. They needed something."

"Yes, I agree. And they all have been doing a lot better." The kids are quiet and being pretty still as Lila slipped something into their drinks with dinner, a little cough medicine to make them crash out.

"They are quieter than I've ever seen them," Lola agrees.

"Jeff asked me out for the weekend. I could really use a babysitter this weekend. As you can see, I've been working with the kids a lot. They're not problems anymore. I don't suppose you'd have pity on me and keep them?"

"I don't know."

"I've gotta get out of the house, Lila. I'm going nuts in there. And I've been working with the kids to make them better. It's only for a couple of nights. Please, I'm begging you. You have no idea what it's like to be stuck in the house with three little kids all the time."

"You're right. That's because I've planned it that way."

"But look at them, Lila. They're your nieces and nephew. How can you turn these little cuties away?"

"Aw, they are acting lots better. Sure, I'll do it."

Sucker!

Chapter 7.2. Time Stealing

People who don't respect your time make life so much more difficult than it has to be. Doing what they want puts what you've got to do on the back burner. It doesn't mean it deletes what you have to do, you've just got to do it a lot later is all.

"I'm going to run some errands, Tony. I'll be back in an hour or so."

"Oh, let me go too. I've got a few things I need to do too, Iris."

Iris is happy to give him a ride, and the two take off. "I've got to drop books off at the library, go to the pharmacy to pick up a script, then I wanted to pick up something for dinner before heading home. What do you have to do?"

Tony gets a phone call; he holds up one finger. "Hello. Oh, sure, I can do that. Yes, I'm in town now. I'll let you know when I've got it done. Bye. Can you take me to the hardware store really quick?"

"Ok." Off they go to the hardware store where Tony spends an hour getting things.

Back in the car, they go, and Tony looks at the time. "Oh, shoot. It's almost time for the bank to close. Can you take me there now?"

"Sure."

To the bank, they go, and Tony goes inside where he does his banking business then comes out with another guy, and they stand there and talk for another hour as Iris sits in the car, growing more and more impatient as she's done none of her errands.

Tony finally gets into the car. "Did you have to have an hour-long conversation, Tony?"

"Oh, yeah I did. I haven't seen David in years. His mother died a month ago. You can't walk away from a conversation when that's said, Iris. It would be rude. We can go do what you need to do now."

"Gee, thanks."

But they can't go yet as Tony gets another phone call. "You want me to pick up a bale of hay? Sure."

"Um, where are you planning on putting a bale of hay and where are you planning on getting this hay? I'm not even going to ask why you need it or who that was who asked you for it." Lois is steaming mad as she speeds through town to get to the library before it closes, and she's stuck with books that will now be overdue if she misses checking them back in.

"The trunk. You've got a big trunk, Iris. And the hay farm is just outside of town. It'll only take a minute to pick it up. The turn is right up here."

Blowing off her own errands, Iris speeds to take Tony to do whatever he needs to do then get back home where she can drop him off. He's totally stolen her time.

Chapter 7.3. Comparisons

No one likes to be compared to anyone else in a negative way. Sure, if someone says that you remind them of Mother Theresa, you're flattered. If someone says that you remind them of their grumpy old uncle, you're less than flattered.

Bob and Marsha are out on their first date. They met online with a dating app, so they know a lot about what the person wanted to let them know, but little about their real personalities.

Marsha sees Bob as he rides his bike up to the park, she's waiting for him at. "Hi, Bob. It's me, Marsha. It's nice to meet you; face to face."

"Yeah, me too." He gets off his bike and hugs her awkwardly. "Your hair smells like lemons."

"Thanks." She smiles and sits on the bench.

Bob sits down too. "My ex used to use lavender scented shampoo on her hair."

"Oh? Well, I thought we might grab a bite from one of the food trucks around the park. I was waiting for you to get here before I got anything."

"Um, food trucks huh?" He sighs. "My ex was deeply opposed to eating out of those things. She worked for the health department for a short time. She says those trucks are usually unsanitary. Like no hot water or something, I guess."

"So, you'd rather not get anything from them, then? Is that what you're saying?"

"Yeah, that's what I'm saying."

"Okay then. I guess we can take a walk. A few streets over, there's a nice little place. We can go Dutch; I can pay for myself."

"Yeah, okay."

Later, as they order their food, Marsha tells the waitress what she'll have, "The six-ounce filet, medium rare please."

Bob's eyes bug out. "Rare? Really?"

"Medium rare," she corrects him.

"My ex refused to eat anything with any pink in it at all."

"Bob, in case you haven't noticed, I'm not your ex."

"Oh, I know. You've got kind of reddish blonde hair, and she had this thick, lustrous brown. And her eyes were green, and yours are kind of grey."

Marsha gets up with a smile as she looks at the waitress. "You know what, forget my order. I'm leaving. It was a pleasure to meet you, Bob. You're not over your ex though. Good luck and goodbye."

Chapter 7.4. Gaslighting

Gaslighting is the most insidious thing a person can do to another person. This tact of making someone think they are actually going crazy should be illegal.

You might think you'd never fall for this, but people do it all the time. We're all so busy in today's world. There's so much going on around us, the cell phone, the television, the computer, and other people; it can be very distracting. That's why people are being gaslighted more than ever.

It's just a lot easier to do now is why.

Rachel and Paul have been married for a few years. Paul has been feeling a little out of it lately. His wife keeps telling him things that he just doesn't recall. And he's unsure of his memories - period.

"I took the trash out, Rachel." He goes to take a seat on the couch.

"Did you put it in the right dumpster this time?" she asks.

"I put it in the one I always put it in."

"There are three of them out there. I told you that we're supposed to only use the one nearest to our building, the one behind it, not the one in front of it."

"Yeah, and I put it in the one behind us. I remembered."

"Are you sure? I don't want a call from the apartment manager again."

"Look, I just walked in from doing it. I put the damn bag of trash in the right dumpster!"

"No need to get huffy. I was just trying to make sure. You did forget several times in a row. You can't blame me for asking."

Paul sits there, trying to remember when he ever put the trash in the wrong dumpster, and can't remember a time he did it. "Rachel, I don't think I've ever put it in the wrong dumpster. Once you told me about what the manager told you, I've always put it in the back dumpster."

"No, you haven't. You've put it in the one in front five times in this last month. How come you keep forgetting that? I'm really beginning to worry about you."

"I'm beginning to worry about me too then because I don't recall doing that even once."

And Paul isn't wrong. He hasn't done it even once – Racheal just wants him to think he has.

Chapter 7.5. Disappearing Act

This might seem like a weird way to play a mind game with someone, but it happens a lot. The person wants to see if you miss them when you can't talk to or see them.

Mindy and Josh went out on a couple of dates then Mindy just dropped off the face of the Earth. Josh thought they got along well, and he liked her a lot.

He texts and calls, but she never answers. After a week, he stops even trying to contact her; she's obviously not as into him as he thought she was. A day goes by without him trying to contact her; then she's suddenly back in play. "Hey, Josh. I haven't heard from you in a while. I was out of town and accidentally left my phone at home. I saw the messages you left, but then you just stopped leavening them. I hope you didn't think I was blowing you off."

"Um, yeah, I did think that."

"Sorry. I'm such a goof sometimes. I leave my phone off or at home lots of times on accident. So, do all of those missed messages mean that you missed me?"

That's all she ever wanted was for him to miss her. She pulled the stunt to get him to keep thinking about her, and it worked.

Chapter 7.6. Protecting the Image

Narcissists are people who have to have the outside world think they've got it all. Protecting their image must be done all the time and at all costs. So, if someone spots a chink in their highly polished armor, it goes all over them.

Pam makes sure her home is spotless. Her car has to be clean all the time. The yard must be in pristine condition at all times. Heaven forbid anyone sees anything of hers in disarray.

But things aren't going well for Pam today. The toilets have overflowed, and she had to call the plumber who told her the septic tank had to be sucked out.

Having a nasty job like that going on at her home is not what she wants anyone to see. "Oh, well that's terrible. Do you suppose you can come late tonight to empty it out?"

"At night?"

"Yes, we'll be too busy to deal with that during the day. It's best if you come back at night – after dark – to deal with that."

"I don't normally like to work after dark. Overtime is expensive, ma'am. I assure you that you'll want this taken care of sooner rather than later."

Her home did smell like a sewer now that the toilets had backed up. But she could keep people out of her house – she couldn't stop people from driving by her home and witnessing the horror of the septic system being pumped out.

What would people think?

"I'll pay whatever the cost is. Just come and do it after dark. And please try to do it as quickly as possible."

"It's gonna really cost you. You sure?"

She'd avoid anyone seeing that, at all costs. "Yes, I'm sure. I'll go get my checkbook and pay you now. That way you can come after dark and do the job then just leave. No one should be any the wiser if you do it that way."

"Lady, we all have sewers that need to be cleaned out now and then. There's nothing to be ashamed of."

"I'm not ashamed of a thing. Just do as I'm paying you to do."

The lengths someone will go to, to pretend their lives are perfect can be amazing.

Chapter 7.7. Saying No, But Wanting to Say Yes

Playing with people's emotions is a thing everyone does at one time or another. We might not even mean to be doing it, but it happens anyway.

Linda and Luke have been dating for a couple of weeks. One night, the kissing gets a bit out of hand, and both of them want much more.

Linda has been brought up to be a respectable woman though. Sex isn't a thing she's about to do until she's got a ring on her finger. Holding her hand to Luke's chest, she pulls her mouth away from his. "What's wrong, Linda? Don't you want to do this?"

She wants to, very badly. But she can't say that. "No, I don't want to do this. Not yet." She also doesn't want to tell Luke that she won't be doing it until he makes a real commitment to her.

"When?"

"I don't know. I'll know when the time is right, I suppose."

"You sure you don't want to do this. You're body is saying yes."

"No, I don't want to do it."

"Okay then."

Both are disappointed, and it's all because of her lack of honesty that they'll both be frustrated for a while.

Chapter 7.8. Getting Even

While the old – an eye for an eye – saying sounds barbaric, people still follow this concept at times. It's not a positive way to deal with things, but people do it anyway.

Jake and Lola have been dating for a while. Neither of them has made the big commitment to the other yet, so going out with someone else isn't exactly off the table.

When Lola sees Jake out with another woman, she's mad. Instead if telling him how hurt she is and how much she really likes him, she goes out with some other guy and makes sure Jake sees it.

Back and forth they go, until everything they had is gone. And it all could've been avoided, and their relationship saved had Lola just been honest with Jake about how she felt when she saw him with someone else and how she'd like to become exclusive with him.

Chapter 7.9. Keeping Your Options Open

Dating is tricky. There are no set and steadfast rules when it comes to dating. When you go out on your first date, both parties understand they are not exclusive. Both parties can go out with other people without anyone getting angry or hurt by it.

But when you date for a while, the unsaid rule is that you should make at least a small commitment to that person. You shouldn't date anyone else if you're seeing one person pretty regularly.

Keeping your options open for who else might come along might seem smart. But it's really not. You could wait a bit too long, and the one you've got will walk away, tired of waiting for you to stop keeping the door open for someone else to come through – someone who might be better than whom you have now.

Chapter 7.10. DIY Self-Defense Technique

If you experienced any of the things you've read about here, would you give the person a chance to change when you called them out on it? Or would you walk away from them without letting them know you were onto them? Or would you let them know you are on to them and you're done with them? And why?

Conclusion

You've read about a lot of darkness that is in this world in these pages. As much darkness as there is, there is even more light. There is no reason to be worried about anything you've read. You can combat every bit of it.

When you look at it with an informed eye, you can see how simple these techniques of darkness really are. All you have to do is keep your mind alert and be aware of things that make you feel a little uneasy. Don't be afraid to take a few steps back to reevaluate things if you feel you need to. And if anyone gives you trouble about that, then there's even more reason to take your time and to think about things thoroughly before proceeding any further.

Don't worry. You've got this!

The End

Finally, if you enjoyed this book, then I'd like to ask you for a favor. Would you be kind enough to leave a review for this book on Amazon?

It'd be greatly appreciated!

Thank you and good luck!

Made in the USA
Las Vegas, NV
22 January 2022